PETER KREITLER

WITH BILL BRUNS

Affair
Prevention

MACMILLAN PUBLISHING CO., INC.

NEW YORK

COLLIER MACMILLAN PUBLISHERS

LONDON

Where confidentiality is desired, I use
only fictitious names. Any correlation with fact in a
particular person's life is pure coincidence.

Macmillan Publishing Co., Inc.

866 Third Avenue, New York, N.Y. 10022

Collier Macmillan Canada, Ltd.

Library of Congress Cataloging in Publication Data
Kreitler, Peter.
    Affair prevention.
       1. Adultery—United States. I. Bruns, Bill, joint
author. II. Title.
HQ806.K73   306.7'3   80-28866
ISBN 0-02-566710-6

This book is published by special arrangement

with Eric Lasher and Maureen Lasher.

10 9 8 7 6 5 4 3 2 1

Designed by Jack Meserole

Printed in the United States of America

*I would like to dedicate this book to
the nineteen people who were courageous
enough to take my original class on
affair prevention in 1978.*

CONTENTS

ACKNOWLEDGMENTS

It is with deep gratitude that I offer thanks to the many people who have so openly shared their stories with me, for without their candor and honesty this book could not have been written.

Thanks also to my friends Frank and Virginia Davis, Rob and Susie Maguire, and the Sprague-Mingst families who so graciously offered their homes at the beach so that I might have a place near the water to write.

Thanks to Caryl Carothers, Jill Flynn, Judy Pickett, and Bill Worthington who gave invaluable counsel and constructive criticism throughout the project.

Thanks to the staff at St. Matthew's Church for their patience and support.

Thanks to Maureen and Eric Lasher and Toni Lopopolo for their encouragement and their sense of humor as we developed two words into a book.

And most especially, thanks to all the professional counselers, psychiatrists, and clergy who freely offered advice and direction.

Affair
Prevention

CHAPTER 1

The Genesis
of Affair Prevention

"Peter, I'm having this problem, and I need to know what you would do," Rich said. "My girl friend is jealous of my mistress, and I don't know how to handle the situation."

"You'd better fill in some of the details," I replied, not really knowing what to say.

"Well, it's a long story, but I've had a mistress for over a year, and I pay for her apartment and her car. My new girl friend has found out about the arrangement and she wants the same deal, but that's crazy—I can't afford it. She's really giving me a hard time."

At that point I was thinking about Rich's wife, Carla, and their two small children. I was wondering how they fit into this scenario.

"What about Carla?" I asked.

"Oh, don't worry about her. She doesn't know, and it doesn't affect her. I just need some advice on how to handle my girl friend; she's the one who's upset."

In August of 1969, at the end of that decade of political, social, and sexual turmoil, I moved to Kansas City, Missouri, to begin my ministry in the Episcopal Church. My background and schooling to that point was entirely East Coast. I attended prep school in Connecticut and graduated with a B.A. in sociology from Brown University and a Masters in

Divinity from Virginia Theological Seminary. All of this eastern education may have prompted a visit by an elderly parishioner at the end of my first week on the job. He entered my office, asked me to be seated, and then proceeded to assure me that I was now in the *real* America—not an East Coast or West Coast version. He impressed me with his appreciation for the values of Middle America, and as I was to learn over the next five years he was basically correct: Kansas City, which seems representative of the American heartland, stands for strong family, church, and community. I discovered, however, that those qualities did not exempt my parishioners from being human like the rest of us.

I first met Rich, a successful young businessman, at a dinner party given to introduce the new cleryman in town. We enjoyed a long discussion on a mutual interest—sailing— and an immediate bond was kindled. It was a couple of days later that Rich called me at the office and said he needed to talk with me—but not about sailing on Lake Perry. We had a long talk about his "problem." The situation was so complicated and he was trying to deal with it at such an elementary level, by worrying about his girl friend's jealousy, that I felt ill-equipped to work it through with him. So, I referred him to a psychiatrist.

Over my years in Kansas City I counseled many parishioners who were engaged in or affected by extramarital affairs. I dealt with these cases as best I could—some of them easily, others with much more difficulty—yet always with an underlying uneasiness at what I found to be a common theme: *I was always relating with people on an after-the-fact basis and forced to take an after-the-fact approach.* Either the affair was in progress and unknown to the other spouse or it had just come to light and the uninvolved spouse had come to me with a justified need to ventilate feelings. In essence people were telling me, "My marriage is in shambles. Won't you please help me try to save it?"

As I struggled to understand an increasingly common situation in my parish community, I was experiencing difficulty with my own six-year marriage. I became so absorbed in trying to build a reputation in a profession that demanded both time and energy that I found myself drifting from my wife, Edon. At the same time, a young woman came into my life who would begin to absorb even more energy. She initially came to me to discuss tension within her own marriage, yet as we spent time together in my office, we began to realize that our mutual "free spirits" were released in each other's presence, and we started looking for reasons to be together. We were the same age, we saw life in a similar fashion, and we shared a similar hobby—all of which encouraged closer and more frequent contact. All the while we were totally oblivious to the process we were beginning; in our minds we were just good, close friends.

Then one warm spring day, I began to realize I was falling in love with this lady, and the realization came as a shock. Here I was, a productive and well-adjusted young clergyman, married to a beautiful and talented woman, the father of two great children, and a man who was not blind to the power of Eros and the appeal of affairs. I had everything going for me, or so I thought, and yet I was on my way to having an extramarital sexual relationship. "What is going on?" I thought to myself. "What is happening to me? Why have I let myself get into this predicament?"

The euphoria from falling in love, coupled with the confusion I felt, made me an ineffectual father, husband, and minister for many months. Yet like so many men before me, I learned to bluff my way through work and marriage while most of my psychic energies were channeled to this woman in the next town. As the relationship bloomed, I realized I was living exactly the kind of life that I had heard about so often in my office. Although I had not considered any of these men and women to be evil, terrible people, and I certainly did not think of myself as a sinner who should be condemned to the stocks, I was aware of great changes going on within me—changes I wasn't sure I was happy with. I was very conscious that my personal behavior and my well-established values were rapidly going out of sync.

During this period of my infatuation and my withdrawal from my family, my wife began to spend time with a man with whom she had an immediate bond, someone we both knew and respected. The fact that he, too, was married should come as no real surprise. Edon and this man, Harry, began to see each other frequently, and I was so aware of my own feelings and behavior at this point that I could see in her behavior some of the same patterns. I began to be suspicious.

One Saturday night the four of us (Edon, myself, Harry and his wife) found ourselves together at a large dinner dance, and I experienced the pain of watching my wife relate to another man in a manner that signaled more than just friendship: The way they looked at each other and the way they danced and held each other were clear signs that they had developed a level of intimacy.

This brought me face to face with a difficult and delicate decision. My wife had said nothing to me about Harry that indicated any special feelings, yet I debated whether I should confront her with my suspicions or just let them slide and hope I was wrong. I made my decision the next morning as I was walking down the aisle of the church with the rector. I turned to him and said, "I can't tell you why now, but I have to leave to take care of a personal matter." I did an about-face, walked out of the church, took off my robe, got in my car, and drove straight home.

Edon was already there, having attended the early worship service, and the moment I came in the door my first words were, "We need to talk. Something is going on with you and Harry. Are you in love with him?" Somehow that was the most important question to ask at that time. Edon

said, "No, I'm not in love with him." I wasn't convinced, so
we pursued the discussion, but not until the next morning
did she admit, "Yes, I'm falling in love with him." At that
point, I too confessed the strong feelings I had for my lady
friend, and we both opened a window to our extramarital
relationships.

Thus confronted by the perilous state of our marriage,
Edon and I decided to begin the slow process of defusing
the relationship we had with our lovers. Our strong attractions
for these two friends continued to have a powerful hold on us,
and for many months we were in constant tension, but we
never lost our commitment to communicating with each
other and searching for a satisfying reconciliation. Although
the opportunity to have sexual relations with our lovers/
friends had always been there and "going to bed" would have
been an easy process, we fortunately remained faithful to our
belief in sexual fidelity and refused the temptation. Something
held us back, and in retrospect we feel it was a combination of
factors: We felt that sexual intercourse would have made a
clear dividing line between friend and lover, and had we
crossed that line we would have violated vows we had shared
with each other many years earlier.

Something else that helped us save our marriage at that
time was our willingness to admit our mistakes and to try to
learn from them. We candidly shared our mutual stories over
and over again—not to hurt each other or to retaliate, but to
gain a clearer understanding of why we had fallen in love with
another person and why our marriage had taken this turn.
The answers were slow in coming, but the more we talked and
shared our feelings, the clearer the picture became. Con-
siderable outside counseling (individually and as a couple)
also proved invaluable and provided a framework for our
concentrated efforts at saving the marriage. Today, looking
back on that experience we lived through—and survived—
as a married couple, we are not proud of what happened. But

we are pleased that we did not go to bed with the third persons in our lives and that we took the time to evaluate our marriage and our other relationships.

During this process of removing the third person from my life, another significant event occurred that brought me closer to focusing on the concept of affair prevention. A married woman we knew and cared for fell in love with another man and announced that she wanted a divorce. Hearing this news tore Edon and me apart, for we did not want to lose our good friends. We had the kind of friendship with this couple where we shared a vacation house for two weeks every summer, our children were close friends, and even our dogs got along. I valued that relationship, and I tried to help Jenny see that with some professional help she and her husband could perhaps solve the problems. But my counsel was too late; the affair had been going on for over a year, and she no longer cared about salvaging the marriage.

This single event, coming after all my other experiences in Kansas City, both personal and professional, triggered an anger at my inability to help prevent this type of marriage dissolution from happening. Even if that was an unrealistic hope, I could at least develop a counseling approach that would help make people more aware of the inherent dangers of affairs and more determined to deal with the issue *before the fact*. I started studying and researching the subject as much as possible, but an important break-through did not come until 1977, after Edon and I and the children had moved to Pacific Palisades, California, an upper-middle-class community in Los Angeles. I was preparing a series of lectures on affairs that I planned to include in a six-week seminar at my church, St. Matthew's. At the same time, I was beginning to hear of the value of holistic medicine, and it struck me, "Why not take the same approach and the same philosophy in dealing with affairs? If preventive medicine can help protect our physical health, then affair-prevention techniques might successfully guard our marital well-being.

With this concept firmly in mind, all my efforts were directed toward the early detection of a possible affair and the development of a process to work feelings through before the affair happens. From this came a comprehensive look at marriage and affairs, and how, in many instances, they are interrelated. My belief is that marriage is a great deal more than a private agreement between a man and a woman to live together. Society as a whole has an important stake in every marriage—thus in every affair.

CHAPTER 2

Why This Book Is for You

Our image of extramarital affairs is captivating and not easily countered by biblical "thou shall nots," vows of fidelity, or the advice of others. We fantasize about affairs, we kid about them at cocktail parties, and we nod in agreement when we hear people advocating them. Why not? Whether we turn to magazines, novels, television, or movies, affairs are portrayed from one perspective: that they are fun, carefree, and erotic—the tempting response to a boring or troubled marriage.

Affairs can certainly undermine and destroy even the best of marriages, but we tend to deal with problems after-the-fact and have difficulty with the concept of prevention. Add to this society's tacit approval of sexual relationships outside marriage, and it is not surprising that most married people tend to take a "wait-until-it-happens" approach to affairs. Caught up in conflicting emotions when they are first tempted by infidelity, many often put off confronting the developing problem. In many homes, little or nothing is said until *after* one has fallen in love with another person or *after* the affair has come to light and something has to be said. At this point, survival of the marriage is usually in jeopardy, yet this is when counselors are usually called in for help, if they are even sought.

The intent of this book is to help you strengthen your current marriage (or, if you are single or recently divorced, your next marriage) by taking a realistic approach to affairs and addressing important questions. For example, what should you try to do if

- You have heard how prevalent affairs are among your peers, and you want to know why?
- Your best friend is having an affair, and you are bored in your marriage and feel your resolve against adultery is weakening?
- Your counselor has recommended an affair as a way to help your marriage, and you are confused, trying to weigh the potential benefits against the certain risks?
- You have a close extramarital friendship that you want to keep from developing into a sexual relationship—which could unwittingly destroy your marriage?
- You have a good marriage, but you are falling in love with someone other than your spouse?
- You have a strong sense that your spouse is drifting into an affair?
- You are between marriages; an affair broke up your previous marriage, and you want to improve the chances of fidelity by both spouses in your next marriage?
- You have had an affair (or affairs), but you really don't want to have another one?

This book will answer questions like these and many more—not by solely quoting the Scriptures or resorting to moral judgments, but by focusing on the practical techniques of "affair prevention." I will provide an overview of affairs by exploring some of the different types, the positive and negative aspects, and why they happen. I will then describe an approach you and your spouse can take to keep your marriage alive, growing, and much less vulnerable to the seductive appeal of an affair.

If you feel secure in your marriage and are comfortable with your sexual relationship, you may wonder "Why should I worry about affairs? I promised to remain faithful to my spouse, I always have, and I've never even been tempted to cheat." Of course I hope that will remain true forever, but I am convinced that *no marriage is completely immune to the problems or situations that can lead to an affair.* Affairs have always cut across economic, religious, racial, and educational lines; they occur among all people. Immunity is not guaranteed by birth, where we live, social status, or even religious commitment or affiliation. To deny this is to ignore what is happening in this country and negates one of the first steps in prevention: awareness of what is going on around you.

Certainly most affairs are an outgrowth of a weak or deteriorating marriage, but I have also seen strong relationships give way to the power of an affair. Why this happens is difficult to answer and will be explored later in this book, but a happy marriage may not be a guarantee against extramarital relations if one or both partners become complacent or are naive to the appeal of a new acquaintance or the offer of a new body. Most marriages go through difficult times during which the potential for an affair increases.

It is my firm conviction that affair-prevention techniques can provide you with a means to strengthen and, in some cases, ultimately save your marriage. When you decrease the potential for an affair in your marriage, you might very well enhance your chances of remaining happily married into old age.

There are several other reasons for my encouraging all couples, early in the marriage, to deal with the possibility of an eventual affair. I want to start them on an awareness process that love itself does not necessarily conquer all temptation.

· 1. Research has shown that sexual infidelity is the precipitating factor in many divorces, whether the marriage was strong or weak. For example, according to an article in *Medical Aspects of Human Sexuality,* a 1978 survey of 500 psychiatrists showed that 55 percent felt that adultery was a major precipitating factor in divorce. As innocent as affairs might seem on the surface and as pleasurable as they might be for the two lovers, they can affect all of us in a variety of ways: they can break up treasured friendships, tear apart family unity, cause tension within business and community circles, and have a negative impact on the children—who are invariably affected. As a friend wrote, after describing an affair within her circle of friends, "Births, deaths, car pools, vacations, generation gaps have been shared with these friends. Infidelity to one seems somehow to deteriorate the whole."

2. Once an affair gets started and is discovered by the other spouse, the marriage runs into deep trouble. Often the participant in the affair naively assumes that the resulting conflict can be handled in the marriage, yet I find just the opposite usually occurs. There is so much anger, guilt, re-crimination, and revenge-seeking when an affair comes to light that complete reconciliation becomes very difficult.

3. Although many married people are aware of the potential for affairs in their marriage, they usually don't honestly discuss it with their spouse. There is only the implication of sexual faithfulness mentioned in their marriage vows. As a result, most couples tend to overlook what is happening until suddenly one spouse has fallen in love with another person or is sleeping with that person or both. Here again, a rational discussion is hard to come by and the marriage usually remains in great distress.

4. People in basically healthy marriages often get involved in an affair unrealistically hoping or expecting that it will be nothing more than a fleeting liaison or anonymous adultery. Unfortunately, it is not always easy to extricate oneself from an affair; even after the fire of love has been extinguished, the other person can still exert a strong attraction. A casual encounter or transient love affair may result in a continuing relationship that could eventually have a negative impact on the marriage.

5. Couples often go through periods of individual and marital stress that may continue for several years. Although many sources of help are available—ministers, psychiatrists,

marital counselors, etc.—if an affair is seen as the only real solution to the marital difficulties, then counseling may not do much good. An affair generally closes the door on a marriage that is in trouble—slamming it shut.

In terms of affair potential, I think we can put most marriages in a grey area between two extremes. One extreme is the Ivory Snow marriage, in which both partners are happily married and compatible, and fidelity is not even an issue. They are not likely to be affected by cultural trends or even tempted by affairs. Prevention techniques will come to them naturally and easily, simply by the way they live their marriage.

At the other extreme is a marriage in which fidelity is not important and is not an expressed or implied goal for either spouse. Perhaps they have an "open" marriage in which they believe it is good to explore sexual relations with others at any opportunity. Or perhaps the marriage has been a battleground—and a mistake—from the beginning. They have remained together for any of several reasons (e.g., "the kids"), and affairs are a likelihood because they do not really care what happens to their marriage: affair *promotion* is more applicable than affair *prevention*.

These two extremes represent many marriages; however, most fall somewhere in between. We are basically moral people who value our Judeo-Christian heritage and want to make our marriages work. But we are also realistic, and we realize that our marriages need constant attention to ensure long-term health.

Underlying all the flippancy and gamesmanship about affairs there is a basic belief in the value of being faithful. In 1977 a survey by the National Opinion Research Center at the University of Chicago found that 73 percent of the adults questioned said that extramarital sex was "always wrong," 14 percent said "almost always wrong," and only 3 percent said "not wrong at all." Still, to achieve this goal of

fidelity we need mutual encouragement, support, and guidance. Thus, "affair-proofing" our marriage has a particular
appeal, and the way to begin is by better understanding affairs and why they happen.

(I also want to address those of you who are looking for
help *after* an affair has begun in your marriage. You may be
currently involved in an affair but the euphoria has worn off,
leaving you feeling isolated. You still feel you are trapped in
an unfulfilling marriage, and you are looking for some
answers or perspectives to help you cope. Or perhaps your
spouse has just admitted to having an affair, and you are
bitter and confused, wondering how to deal with this news
and where to turn for help. In either case, I feel this book
can help you understand why the affair occurred and what
you and your spouse can learn from the experience that will
help improve your marriage.)

One preconception you may hold is that because I am
an ordained minister in a traditional, institutional church I
am obviously against affairs ("Of course *you* can't go around
advocating them!") and my book will be narrow, ill-informed,
and naive. I therefore want to briefly explain my approach
as a minister and my background as a married man with two
children.

First of all, I try to avoid making dogmatic moral judgments with people I counsel or advise. My basic belief is
acceptance first, change second: "I accept you for who you
are, regardless of your behavior." As a minister and a family
man, I treasure our Judeo-Christian heritage of fidelity and
covenant, the value of the family, taking responsibility for
one's own life, and personally striving for moral actions. I am
not a moralist who says his approach to marriage, with regard
to extramarital affairs, is right for everybody. I am well aware
that your attitude may reflect the thinking of a forty-year-old
housewife in my parish who told me, rather gleefully, "Affair
prevention? Hell, I've been trying to have an affair for years.

I'm just looking for the right man!" Having multiple sexual experiences while you are married, or a single long-term affair, is your choice. In fact, I am willing to admit that for some people, in certain marriage situations, there may be value in an affair for the individual (usually when the other spouse does not know). So I offer an openness on this subject, without apologizing for the religious and moral commitments I have made in my profession and my life.

A second point is that, in my counseling experience, I have not found it helpful to quote Scriptures to most people who are contemplating or having an affair. Fellow clergymen have said to me, "Peter, all you need to do is have people read 1st Corinthians 6:18 ['Flee fornication. Every sin that a man doeth is outside the body, but he who committeth fornication sinneth against his own body'] and Deuteronomy 22:22 ['If a man is caught having intercourse with another man's wife, both of them are to be put to death. In this way you will get rid of this evil']." It is comforting to know that many people still find great strength in the moral proscriptions of the Bible, and it would be helpful if a knowledge of what the Old Testament and Jesus had to say about adultery were internalized and could keep all of us from having affairs. Unfortunately, the Bible's teachings are often seen as an outdated part of a hard-line moralistic approach to life that needs revision for life in the twentieth century. And the teachings on sexuality in particular are seen by some as downright archaic, or at best unrealistic.

Therefore, disciplines such as sociology and psychology, as well as religion, have contributed to my understanding of affairs. I have found that to be of help to people having affairs, I need to be in touch with more than just the Bible.

Third, I have learned from experience that being a minister does not exempt one from being part of the human race. My profession is considered one of the most moral of professions, yet clergymen are as susceptible as everybody else to having an affair. Even though they affirm belief in

God, subscribe to the ten commandments, and have strong
religious commitments, these men and women, with positions
of power and influence in the religious community, have
affairs. The revelation of these affairs, in some communities,
has cost them their jobs and their marriages. This is no
startling revelation if your image of the ministry was created
by Elmer Gantry and the jokes about the minister running
off with the choir director, leaving church, family, and
friends behind. This is no laughing matter to the clergy, however, for such jokes strike too close to home.

When counseling people who are going through an
affair or contemplating one, I am not simply a sideline com-
mentator—a Monday-morning quarterback—trying to take
the "fun and intrigue" out of married life by talking about
affair prevention. As I noted earlier, I have experienced falling in love with another woman during my marriage, and I
know how easily you can be drawn into an affair—even if you
have a relatively happy marriage guided by religious beliefs.

Out of my personal and counseling experiences has come
the conviction that *when we work on "affair prevention," we
reaffirm the belief that a marriage based on fidelity and the
vow that it will never be broken is a worthwhile goal and a
way of life that can bring great satisfaction.* For better or
worse, most of us commit ourselves to marriage in the hope
that we can maintain a lifelong union and a balance of *heart*
(authentic love), *body* (mutually satisfying sexual relations),
and *mind* (shared interests, goals, and activities). This is a
lofty ideal which we may not meet; we may succumb to the
pressures and temptations along the way. But we can hope
that after thirty or forty or fifty years together we can proudly
say "I would like to do that all over again." And I hope this
book helps you affirm that belief.

CHAPTER 3

Types of Affairs

Technically, I could substitute the word adultery for affair throughout this book, since both experiences include— by my definition—the same thing: voluntary sexual intercourse between a married person and someone other than his or her spouse. But my main focus is on affairs because most of them entail more than just adultery, thus posing a greater threat to most marriages.

I view adultery as an act of intercourse rather than a continuing relationship. It is often a brief encounter between two persons who may never see each other again, sex for the sake of sex. *By contrast, more than just sex is involved in most affairs.* There is usually an intense emotional involvement with the lover; the relationship grows or continues over a period of weeks, months, or even years; and energy is drained from the marriage. This is an affair with a capital A.

Extramarital relationships—both adulterous and non-sexual—can destroy the best of marriages. It might be a one-night stand at a Chicago convention between two persons who meet, share drinks and dinner conversation, make love, and part company forever. Or it could be an emotional or intellectual friendship that lasts for months or even years without sex ever occurring. However, I have found through my experience and research that an affair is potentially much more threatening and damaging to marriage than either of the above situations.

Affairs result from such a variety of extramarital relationships that I want to first isolate and explore the common types, giving you greater insight into the potential situations that can arise in any marriage. In doing so, I will draw on case studies and illustrative quotes from my professional experience that represent some universal truths about affairs. It is likely that you will identify feelings you have had during your marriage and perhaps some similar situations—if not in your own marriage, then vicariously through close friends. That is my intent: to help you get in touch with the varying emotions and experiences in an affair. *Prevention starts here, with an awareness of the temptations, pitfalls, myths, and realities of affairs.*

The Friendship Affair

A great blues song written about fifty years ago warns: "Don't you worry about strangers, keep an eye on your best friend." This is still poignantly true today, for most affairs develop among people we already know, such as good acquaintances, social and sporting friends, fellow club members, and co-workers. Few of us are comfortable developing immediate intimacy or quick friendships; we shy away from letting others know us unless they are our friends. So it is logical to assume that among our good acquaintances are persons of the opposite sex we especially like—for their openness, honesty, looks, interests, or whatever—and we choose to be with them, as friends. *However, in this network of friendships is often a person with whom an affair has great appeal.*

One common breeding ground exists in established neighborhoods where there is a relatively low turnover of families and a lot of interaction in backyards and living rooms. Here is where marriages can be especially vulnerable in times of marital stress or personal turmoil.

In Kansas City, I counseled one couple in particular whose marriage was undermined by a classic friendship affair. Two young families lived next door to each other, and all four adults were good friends, as were their seven children.

One husband, Steve, traveled a lot in his job while the other husband, Michael, worked at home as an insurance agent. Michael and his wife, Doris, had a large barbecue pit and an attractive backyard, and they frequently invited the next-door neighbors over for dinner. If Steve happened to be out of town, his wife, Nancy, would go over with the kids anyway. Later in the evening, when the kids were in bed, the adults would sit around, drinking wine and talking. The wife of the insurance agent, Doris, needed more sleep than her husband, so she would go to bed earlier, often leaving her husband alone with Nancy. Doris never had any suspicion that trouble was brewing: Nancy was her best friend, and she trusted the relationship they had built over the years. Nevertheless, Michael and Nancy began to talk about their marriages when they were alone (Michael's wife in bed, Nancy's husband off traveling), and they admitted that their marriages were missing a spark. Over time, they found the spark in each other. Thus began an affair that would lead to two divorces and a marriage between two neighbors.

As one might expect, the lives of the adults as well as the kids were dramatically altered. Steve, the non-involved traveling husband, was relatively unshaken by the turn of events; his life continued to be wrapped up in his job (though he began to spend more quality time with his kids than ever before). But Doris, the non-involved wife, was devastated, especially since hers was a double loss: her husband and her best friend. She left town with her children.

Meanwhile, Michael and Nancy married and continued to live in the same neighborhood, but her children were understandably confused by "adult" behavior. Their father (Steve) moved out and the next-door neighbor moved in— an adult who had been their friend was now their parent— but on weekends they stayed with their father.

This is an example of the friendship affair that so often happens with neighbors, although the specific details may not be known. Cherished friendships give way to unanticipated love affairs, and the friendships are often lost forever. Later in the book, I will talk specifically about how to maintain healthy extramarital friendships in ways that are natural, fun, and designed to help prevent falling in love.

The Be-a-Good-Neighbor Affair

This is a variation of the friendship affair pattern. Many of us want to be the Good-Samaritan neighbor, and when a member of the opposite sex is hurting and wants to talk about his or her troubled marriage, we naturally want to try to help. But one "unloading" session may lead to another, and a good friendship can sometimes develop into something more intimate than was originally intended.

Here is one common way this type of affair can start. A thirty-six-year-old man, an advertising executive, was talking with a lady friend at a neighborhood Fourth-of-July party, and she started telling him about the problems she was having in her marriage. He admitted that he wasn't having a very happy time at home either. At the conclusion of their long chat, she suggested, "Why don't we go out some night and talk about it?" My friend felt it was a good idea at the time ("I thought I could help her and she could help me"), but after dinner, discussion, and drinks they ended up going to bed together that night, and a sexual affair began. They called it off several months later, before it came to light and could destroy their marriages, but their friendship was over also and they were no longer good neighbors.

There is also the example provided by Jack and Cindy, both thirty-eight and married eleven years. Through his community activities Jack met a woman who had been married for nearly twenty years and who lived just a few miles away. He saw her at several meetings, and they occasionally had dinner or lunch together. "I like to look at other women," he told me, "but I've got everything I want; no guy with what I have would be looking for an affair." Yet he let himself get involved with this woman. "She took the initiative. She told me she was having trouble at home and that she really needed somebody to listen to her. I'm such a nice guy that I tried to help. I never dreamed anything would happen between us; she caught me totally off guard. I was a savior image for her, and she began stroking my ego, saying things I wanted to hear. I began to realize something was happening, but I liked what she was saying, even though my wife had said the same things many times."

In Jack's view, to be a good neighbor meant listening, caring, and supporting this woman. He believed in the golden rule and he wanted to help, so it was natural to become involved. But friendships are special and are well worth preserving, and we must be careful not to risk damaging these relationships by being unaware of the appeal our friends can have.

The Cup-of-Coffee Affair

Many affairs begin innocently enough over a cup of coffee, a cup of tea, or a drink between fellow workers or hobbyists (e.g., the midmorning break in the Lever Brothers building in New York or the night class in landscape architecture at UCLA). The offer "How about a cup of coffee?" is usually a polite, thoughtful gesture, and I certainly do not wish to discourage this type of interaction between men and women. However, we all should be aware of where this situation may lead. Dr. Roger Gould, a well-known Los Angeles psychiatrist and an astute observer of human behavior, told me, "Once you've shared a cup of coffee, it may already be in your mind that down the road it's going to be more than a cup of coffee." I would add: *if you share coffee, you may—consciously or unconsciously—already be "toying" with the idea of an affair.* That is a strong statement, but it is intended to be just that.

Here is a typical example. Wendy, a twenty-eight-old

married hospital administrator, started spending her coffee breaks with a fellow worker named Doug. "We'd just sit and talk about innocent little things, but I felt so good I found myself wanting to spend more time with him. He was sensitive to my needs, and he seemed to understand me better than my husband did. Pretty soon, we were having lunch together, and before I knew it I was in love with him."

Another illustration is provided by Trudy, age thirty-two, who had been married six years. Because she was increasingly dissatisfied with being a housewife, she started taking night courses at the University of California. In one class she met an attractive, older, mature man who appealed to her. "I was very aware of his sitting next to me," she said. "It was raining one night and he offered his umbrella as we left. He also offered to buy me a cup of coffee, and I accepted." The cups of coffee they shared began a process of deepening communication that felt terrific, and although she was aware of what was happening to her very early in the game, she continued to play. When she came to me for advice, we talked about the pros and cons of this affair, but I knew—and she knew—that she was going to succumb. "My traditional views on marriage tell me I shouldn't mess around," she admitted, "but what I'm feeling about him usually leads to a sexual relationship. It feels so good it can't be wrong." Sure enough, her decision was to go ahead and pursue the relationship, letting "what happens, happen." Her husband eventually discovered the affair, and when she flaunted it by going off on a business trip with her lover, he initiated a divorce.

The Seize-the-Moment Affair

Many of us will find ourselves in a position during our marriage where the opportunity for a brief "no one will ever know" affair is temptingly easy. It might be a typical one-night stand while attending a convention or taking a business

trip—a sexual adventure with little or no emotional attachment. Or it might be "vacation adultery," as described by
Linda Wolfe in her book *Playing Around*. "Everyone
around the place seemed so free, so loose and frivolous in the
sun," she quoted one woman as saying. "Even the water was
sensual. The kids were occupied and I felt free." In this type
of affair, immediate judgments are made and a "what the
hell" attitude overrides the discretion one might have used at
home. The timing is right, the atmosphere is perfect, and it is
presumed no one will ever know.

One young married woman told me how her summer
fling came about. She was alone with the kids in a summer
cabin in Maine for the month of July while her husband
continued working in Boston. Although she was generally
happy with her marriage, she was lonely during these nights
and wanted some adult companionship. So she enrolled in
evening art classes at the recreation center, and her latent
interest in watercolor painting was stimulated by her instructor. At the end of the month, she invited him over for
dinner with the kids to thank him. She had proper intentions
when the evening began, but after the kids went to bed, she
and the instructor settled down in the living room, and they
finished the bottle of wine by candlelight. They talked and
talked and talked—until she invited him into her bed. It
was a special way of saying thank you.

Brief as this sexual encounter was, I would not call the
evening they spent together a one-night stand. It would have
been if this woman had gone to a bar that night, met the art
instructor for the first time, and then gone to bed with him.
But that is not what I am talking about when I refer to vacation adultery or seize-the-moment affairs. The woman may not
have been in love with the fellow, but her energy had been
directed to him for several weeks, and she felt an emotional
attachment. So it was natural for the physical part to evolve
from that relationship.

The Old-Acquaintance-Never-Be-Forgot Affair

Although this type of affair is not as common as the ones I have already discussed, it carries an alluring mystique and is perhaps the easiest to kindle. Most of us occasionally fantasize about that one lover with whom we never really said goodbye or the one that circumstances prevented us from pursuing. During those five or ten or twenty years of separation from that old friend, we remember the good times, and we dream of what might have been and what might be.

Then, by chance or design you meet that old boyfriend or girl friend, perhaps at a high school or college reunion, and it feels as though nothing ever came between you. You reminisce, you laugh about long-ago incidents, and everything is perfect—*if you can avoid that next step.* Most people who "retouch" delight in the experience and put to rest the "old flame," realizing it's best not to rekindle it. Yet there are those who wish to live out the fantasy, and when that old acquaintance resurfaces by calling and saying "I'm passing through— would you like to get together?" they are drawn into a situation that needs careful attention. Some of those who have received this call have gone to dinner, then to bed, and eventually to a divorce court. No one really wants the tension of being in love with someone else while married, but a night in bed together or a fleeting romance is an appealing prospect with that "old acquaintance."

Joan is a prime example here. Married fifteen years and feeling neglected by a husband who was embroiled in his business and organizations, she went alone to her high school reunion, where she happened to meet an old boyfriend. "He looked so much younger than I imagined he would, and all my old feelings came flooding back," she said. He was equally vulnerable, having just gone through a divorce, and they spent most of the evening together visiting with their old friends.

"The next weekend my husband was out of town, so I called up my friend and we went on a picnic. He brought a bottle of wine, the weather was glorious, and we just sat and held each other, reminiscing about all the good times we had together years ago. Believe me, the temptation to go back to his apartment was very tough to handle, but I managed to keep my head. Now I don't know how much longer I can resist. I've become addicted to this guy again. I keep thinking that we were 'right' and I let him go." At the time we talked her commitment was to her marriage, especially her three children, and she admitted she felt guilty just contemplating an affair. "I'm a religious person, and I never thought I'd have all these feelings about somebody else once I was married." Part of my counsel was to warn her that if she was guilty about her *feelings*, then to act on them could prove disastrous to her self-esteem, as well as her marriage.

The People-Helper Affair

People-helpers, such as doctors, psychiatrists, social workers, counselors, lawyers, and clergy are trained—and generally committed—to helping people cope with difficult personal problems. The nature of the job itself brings helpers into constant touch with people who openly trust them and are willing to reveal their innermost thoughts and emotions. In fact, people-helpers are often viewed as larger-than-life figures who have magical powers to "heal" a person physically, psychologically, or spiritually. As this atmosphere of trust and acceptance grows, through frequency of contact, the intimate nature of the relationship can produce a high potential for affairs, where either the patient, client, or parishioner falls in love with the helper, or vice versa.

As an example, a handsome forty-five-year-old medical doctor told me how a woman fell in love with him and he failed to read the messages she was giving out over several months. He had a troubled marriage of his own and did not recognize the unconscious signals of availability that he, too, was projecting. When he finally realized what was happening, he chose not to discourage an affair with the woman.

In my own profession, clergy are often called upon for their aid in bringing wholeness to fragmented lives and marriages. People *want* to trust rabbis, ministers, and priests. After all, if you can't trust a clergy person, who can you trust? Unfortunately, men and women of the cloth fall in love and have affairs just like everyone else. When their resolve weakens or discretion is cast aside, then the chances for an affair increase greatly. A good perspective is provided by a fellow minister who has been happily married for fifteen years. "If I were to give conscious signals during my counseling that I was 'available,' I could get as much sex as I wanted. Like any clergyman, I counsel women at very vulnerable times in their lives. They come to my office and say 'Nobody loves me . . . I'm not good . . . I don't have an identity.' If I didn't have control of my sexuality, I would not be a good counselor."

More than any other professionals in our society, people-helpers must possess an internal reservoir of resolve to remain at a distance from the people they counsel. If they allow themselves to be seduced by the intimacy of one-to-one professional relationships, they negate their ability to help and undermine their own code of ethics.

The Western Affair

There are married men who consciously pursue women with the expressed purpose of "scoring." Like the cowboys in old westerns who cut notches in the stock of their guns after they killed a bad guy, these men keep count of their sexual conquests. Women, in their view, are objects to conquer and possess—until someone more attractive or desirable comes on the scene. Each affair seems to represent a notch on the masculinity belt, and it is not unusual for them to boast about their "scores." A fifty-year-old married man from Tucson assured me, with a great deal of pride in his voice, that he dated women only between the ages of nineteen and thirty-three. He was a charming, fun-loving man who in his twenty-four years of marriage had managed to have more than 100 extramarital sexual encounters. In my experience of interviewing, counseling, and reading, this would certainly place him at the high end of the western-affair spectrum, and we might call him a cowboy riding the range.

Men involved in this type of affair are often adept at rationalizing their behavior. I have talked with women who have had affairs with men like this, and they marvel at how well these men explain away their actions with a glib "So what else is new?" One stylish single woman in her late thirties who has enjoyed several affairs with married men states: "A lot of men who are successful in their careers see an affair as their right and their reward. Their attitude is 'I work hard, I make a lot of money, my wife has a beautiful house and an expensive car, we take nice vacations, and I spend time with my kids.' In their view this justifies having a mistress, lover, or one-night stand. Some of them also see it as the 'in' thing to do, a form of status among their peers."

Men riding the range are often looking for single women whose lives are not complicated by kids, PTA meetings, and responsibilities around the home. An executive I know who travels frequently refers to these women not as mistresses but as part of his "traveling squad." "I'm the ideal husband around Los Angeles," he told me, "but anything goes when I'm on the road." But since he doesn't like to go out searching for female companionship in strange cities he has several women in Los Angeles who are ready to travel with him at a moment's notice. "I'll call one of them up on Tuesday morning and say, 'I'm going to Honolulu tonight and I'll be back Friday. Do you want to go?' She sits around the pool during the day while I go about my business, then we go out and have a good time that night."

This type of affair has been almost exclusively in the male domain. Only occasionally have I encountered or heard of married women pursuing men with the same scorekeeping philosophy (e.g., "groupies" who target rock stars, ball players, politicians, or movie stars for the expressed purpose of "sleeping with a celebrity"). However, a similarity of sexual styles will probably become more common as married women gain the freedom to be as sexually exploratory as men have been.

The Office Affair

Whenever people work in close proximity over a period of time, there is a possibility that this intimacy may lead to an affair. Although this affair can happen anywhere, I will use the office situation to illustrate it.

Most people heading for the office in the morning are intent on looking good, working hard, and putting their best foot forward, so much so that the immediate attraction based on clothes, style, and outward appearance is often accentuated in the office. In the *Los Angeles Times*, Suzanne Adelson writes that ". . . the Big Boss shows up each morning showered and shaved and smelling like Ireland's moors, or whatever, and he radiates power. He is also on his best behavior—polite, thoughtful, paternal, debonair. . . ." And to be fair, there is the female executive who also shows up at the office with every hair in place, makeup artfully applied, and smelling like a night on the Nile.

In many instances, going from home to office is a welcomed escape from a troubled marriage into an atmosphere of acceptance and understanding. One young advertising executive admitted that he was ripe for an affair at work because his wife was always tearing him down. "At the office I'm a hero—everybody likes me," he said. "But when I go home, my wife gives me the needle whatever I do. In her eyes I'm not even adequate to take out the garbage."

The time factor is another important reason so many affairs take place in the office. Not only do men and women spend a lot of time working together, but they have a lot of idle time together. As I noted earlier in the "cup-of-coffee" affair, people very often discover a listening ear in a fellow worker of the opposite sex and discuss problems with spouse and kids on a regular basis.

One young real-estate salesman who has been in several offices during his eight-year tenure declared that "real estate is very conducive to affairs. It breeds both alcoholism and adultery because there is a lot of free time, time to talk and complain about spouses, commiserate, and go out to lunch and have drinks." Many offices become centers of personal-problem dialogues, and the dynamics can easily lead to extramarital involvement. How often we hear the boss saying, "My secretary really listens to me—she understands me better than my wife."

CHAPTER 4

Why Prevention, Not Promotion

If I honestly felt that extramarital affairs could enliven and strengthen marriages, my energies would be directed toward promoting them rather than preventing them. This would certainly keep me in step with the advocates of "open marriage" and those who urge us to get what we can out of life. But as carefree, erotic, and appealing as affairs may appear, and despite the benefits they might bring to an individual along the way, I firmly believe most affairs should be prevented from taking place, for several practical, emotional, and social reasons.

It is true that I will offer some enticing reasons why a person contemplating an affair might want to proceed—with caution. In fact, whatever the eventual outcome of an affair, some individuals—and perhaps their marriage as well—may benefit along the way. I will highlight these presumed and real benefits below, but first, *it is important to put the arguments on behalf of affairs in perspective.* I have found, for example, that proponents generally fall into three categories: 1) those who are still experiencing the initial, euphoric phase of being in love, which is felt in nearly every affair, 2) those who were not—or haven't yet been—caught, and 3) those who have not had an affair but are convinced it is the answer to a dull and unrewarding marriage. All of these people will readily extoll the virtues of affairs to anyone who

will listen, but I find that these judgments need to be carefully appraised.

The basic question always remains: *Is the enjoyment
promised by an affair worth all the risks involved?* There are
exceptions, of course, but the participants in an affair must
eventually return to earth and confront the many problems
that arise from their extramarital involvement. To many
individuals living in the "me generation," the presumed
benefits are enough justification for an affair, even if it leads to
a broken marriage and has a painful impact on the other
people involved. Most of those who have been through the entire experience would argue differently, but the decision is
ultimately yours to make—I hope after weighing all the data
you can acquire.

THE BLOOM WILL FADE

First of all, in weighing the pros and cons of affairs it is
important to judge them against the complete experience.
*Almost without exception, affairs are acclaimed during the
initial stages.* Almost everyone is swept away by the power of
new love because "it feels so good." A typical insight is provided by a thirty-nine-year-old stockbroker I know who was
in the formative stage of his affair after sixteen years of
marriage. He talked with the euphoria of a college sophomore
as he told me, "Isn't it terrific, the feeling of young love again?
Wow, it's fabulous." Indeed, there is nothing as uplifting
as that feeling of being in love, and it is not surprising that
most pro-affair statements are made during this initial stage
before the reality of the situation sinks in. Songs, literature,
movies, and personal conversations abound with examples of
how great people feel when they are "madly in love." Time
and time again the familiar words are repeated: "I've never
felt this for someone before; it must be love." The next step
is easy and comes naturally—rationalizing the affair because,
as one of my parishioners told me early in her affair, "I
feel so good, it can't be wrong; it must be right."

THE QUESTION OF DISCOVERY

When seeking information about affairs, I feel it is crucial to listen carefully to those who have had a chance to realistically assess their affair—either after it has been discovered by their spouse or after it is over. Despite the image we like to have, affairs are seldom everlastingly spontaneous, happy, and joyful. The heightened emotional state of being in love gradually dissipates, and the hour of reckoning eventually comes for everyone involved. Even those who get away with their affair over an extended period of time must confront the reality of the experience.

The issue of discovery is very important. I have known several people who have had affairs for a year or longer and have thought they were wonderful experiences, but they overlooked one crucial fact: *They were never caught.* They had home, security, children—plus a secret romance on the side; obviously they were going to be inclined to think that affairs are terrific. But if their affairs had been brought into the open and fully understood by their spouse, the resulting repercussions could easily have left them shaken and ready to exclaim their misfortune rather than their fortune.

A typical example of this realization was provided when I appeared on the Carole Hemingway KABC radio talk show in Los Angeles. One caller informed me that he had enjoyed a variety of affairs during his eleven-year marriage, and he insisted he had a good marriage, to which I responded with a simple question: "Does your wife know of your affairs?" "Of course not," he replied. I asked, "What would happen if she knew?" "She'd kick me out of the house," he said.

The fact that the affair is known by only one partner is a common admission by those who talk glowingly about their "successful" affairs. In fact, I have yet to have one person say to me, "The affair turned out really well for everyone concerned," when it became known by their spouse. Perhaps, if everybody had the power and the willingness to easily forgive and forget, affairs wouldn't be a problem in our culture; we could all move from one liaison to another, according to our whims. Yet in real life the discovery of an affair usually triggers strong and bitter feelings of mistrust, anger, recrimination, and at times hopelessness within the marriage. Once a person has been stunned by the discovery or revelation that his or her spouse has had or is having an affair, the resulting bitterness, sense of ego-deflation, and loss of trust leads in many cases to an irreconcilable situation. The injured spouse can feel justifiably betrayed, for what was once pledged as a sacred vow in the wedding ceremony has been violated. Once this trust has been undermined, the marriage may hang together through patching and mending, but only rarely will it be made whole again, for there is always a lingering resentment and an inability to fully trust the guilty person again. The question is always there: "If I've been cheated on once, can I ever trust my spouse again?"

Meanwhile, *once the truth comes out about an affair, a wrenching reassessment process begins.* Couples are forced to decide if they wish to continue the marriage—knowing that one person has broken the marriage vows—or dissolve the union and move out and on to new relationships. Neither alternative is very appealing to most people caught in this situation, and both partners find themselves confronted with what may be the most devastating period of their life together. Even when the marriage has been unsatisfactory for many years, the discovery and subsequent "discussion" of an affair provokes powerful emotions, because it is a tangible reminder of just how bad the marriage has been. Questions are raised that must be dealt with: "Where to turn? What to do? Who's to blame? Why did it happen?" Most of us are ill-prepared and ill-equipped to face these questions or to answer them.

THE PLEASURE-PAIN PRINCIPLE

The third reason I like to know all the facts about an affair stems from Voltaire's observation that "illusion is the first of all pleasures." He may not have been thinking about affairs when he said that, but I continually discover that *the most vigorous, convincing opponents of affairs are those who have had them.* Jarred by their experience, they have found for themselves that the pleasure an affair might actually bring is almost always balanced or outweighed by the painful moments that result. This point was brought home by a prominent New England doctor in his early sixties who had enjoyed a "successful" affair eight years earlier and was still maintaining a healthy, intimate relationship with this woman long after his marriage had broken up. But when I pressed him to advocate affairs, he would not endorse either them or his behavior. Instead, he said he wished he could replay those events of eight years ago and change his behavior. His affair had brought too much destruction to his family, especially his wife of twenty-five years, and to his relationship with his children and grandchildren.

A fifty-year-old building contractor in Los Angeles, who had had several affairs during his marriage and whose wife left him for another man, offers another example of the pleasure-pain principle that occurs in nearly all affairs. "Sure, an affair is fun," he said. "It was always a big ego trip for me. But in retrospect, there is no real benefit. I know a lot of people who have had affairs, and all of them have ended up divorced. One guy even told me, 'An affair is fun until someone falls in love—then it's agony.' That's how I felt. It's one thing to make love to another person when there's not much emotional attachment; I could live with that. But to fall in love with this other person when you're already married is a terrible frustration and torture."

The Promise of Affairs

An awareness of the pleasure-pain principle leads us to a more complete discussion of the promise and the cost offered by an affair. I will first explore the benefits people feel they have gained through an affair, whatever the eventual outcome of their marriage.

AN AFFAIR INFLATES THE EGO

Perhaps the most common claimed benefit derived from an affair is the boost it can give to self-esteem. We live in an era when we tell one another that a sense of self-assurance and self-worth is critical to our happiness. If we have been starved for "ego strokes" from our spouse, it can be a wonderful feeling to receive them from a secret lover. When this other person finds you appealing, tells you so, and then pursues an intimate relationship, you immediately have good feelings about yourself, which have perhaps lain dormant or have not been reinforced for many years.

An attractive thirty-eight-year-old preschool teacher in Los Angeles, who had a four-year affair prior to the dissolution of her marriage, spoke for many when she told me, "When you get into an affair, it feels so good you let it carry you. I had a change of personality. I was no longer tired all the time, my adrenaline was flowing, and my system was working differently. I lost weight. Even my night clothes became important because someone was noticing. I just stood there and he thought I was neat." Many of us are like this woman, hungering for someone to say we are "neat" just because of who we are. *Affairs, like the courtship before a marriage, thrive early on because both partners are generally very comfortable massaging one another's egos regularly.* Affair lovers spend hours telling each other how wonderful, how special, how loving, and how understanding they are.

Several professional counselors have told me of many situations in which their patients' self-worth eroded during their marriage. This change was at the root of much of their marital discord, and in some cases these same individuals came away from their affair with a renewed sense of confidence and purpose. A psychiatrist and sex therapist I know, who is certainly not an advocate of affairs, told me that "an affair can help a person's self-esteem. The feedback we get about ourselves in a marriage is unique, and so constant and intense, that sometimes it is possible for a partner to feel absolutely crushed. Under these circumstances, an affair can provide a great boost to self-worth." This need to feel needed, accepted, and loved is great in all of us, and when that special person comes into our lives—especially during the vulnerable times in our marriage—and makes us feel like a new person, it is hard to say no to a continuing relationship.

"I'M SEXUALLY OK"

A common but understandable revelation in many discussions about affairs is how they can break down sexual inhibitions and increase sexual confidence. Our culture places a lot of emphasis on being sexually competent and responsive, and this kind of pressure can send some people outside their marriage to discover or reawaken aspects of their sexuality that have been submerged or thwarted in their marriage.

In Kansas City, for example, I counseled a woman in her late forties who described herself to me as an ugly duckling who had been made beautiful by a brief sexual encounter with a long-time friend. She related how, over a period of years, her husband had gradually withdrawn his sexual attention and thus reinforced her "ugly" feelings about herself. Finally, she turned to her friend for more than just conversation and companionship. Their love-making sessions in a Route 66 motel reaffirmed her sexual worth, and she was able to bring a greater sense of spontaneity and responsiveness back into her own marriage. Her husband fortunately responded to this new-found sexual aggressiveness, and she was able to end the sexual relationship with her friend. As she put it, "My friend and I realized that if we continued the sexual part, we would not only jeopardize our marriages but our friendship as well."

My psychiatrist friend also points out that some people have specific sexual problems or perceived dysfunctions that go unresolved until an affair illustrates that the trouble is an emotional, not a physical, disability. One clear illustration of this comes from the experience of a successful trial attorney, who told me that he and his wife had settled into an infrequent sexual routine and that he had begun to experience a decline in desire and partial impotency. "My wife had basically neglected me for the better part of three years," he said. "She didn't respond to me. Then suddenly, I met this woman at work who wanted me as much as I wanted her. Before this affair, I had doubts about myself sexually. Whenever my wife and I made love, she seldom was satisfied and I kept thinking, 'Am I a lousy lover—is that the problem?' But then I had this long-term affair and a couple of office quickies, and it was good for my sexual ego. I found out that I am a good lover. I've always enjoyed women and it made me feel good because they all went away with smiles." The attorney's impotence disappeared with a loving touch that had been absent so long from his marriage. Thankfully, he was able to "reintroduce" himself to his wife with confidence in his sexual ability and she responded with a greater eagerness for sex.

Women can have similar attitudes, feelings, and experiences. There is an inordinate amount of pressure on women to be orgasmic, competent sexual partners, and they are often pressured to be free and spontaneous. One woman who had not had an orgasm during the ten years of her marriage became orgasmic with a younger lover and was happy to tell me about her sexual liberation. "If you can't have sex with your husband," she confided, "you feel dysfunctional. In my marriage, sex was a 'have to,' not a 'want to'; it hurt and it wasn't worth the effort. But if you have good sex with someone else you feel fantastic. You have proved to yourself that you can do it—wow!" Fortunately her affair was brief and she was able to bring her new-found sexual ability and confidence into the marriage.

AFFAIRS CAN HELP MEET TH E
SUPPLEMENTAL NEEDS PEOPLE HAVE
IN A MARRIAGE

Men and women through the ages have justified affairs by declaring that such a relationship "balances" their marriage. Indeed, much of an affair's appeal is that more than sexual needs are usually met. "An affair gives you the chance to know another woman intimately, not just physically but mentally," said Matt, a twice-married but now single art dealer. "I like women and I like to draw them out. Affairs gave me a chance to do this, because you can only stay in bed so long. After a while, you're sharing this person's life and she's sharing yours. You're learning about her in a very special way."

There is a fine distinction here. Wives and husbands can seldom satisfy all the differing needs they each bring to a marriage, and it is unrealistic and unfair for them to have such an expectation. Yet we are social beings, and we have a need to relate to other men and women and to open ourselves up to new experiences, new friendships, new ideas, and new ways of growing. Unfortunately, this truth is frequently misunderstood and abused. For example, Archie begins to delight in the attributes of Veronica to the exclusion of his wife, Betty, and the secondary relationship replaces the primary one. Or a wife might argue, "My husband never shows any interest in my painting or gives me any support. He just can't understand me. So I feel completely justified in finding someone else who will share my interest." In and of itself, this is of value, and I encourage men and women to cultivate and nourish extramarital *friendships*. However, the supplemental sex that may eventually accompany these relationships changes the ground rules, and that is what I try to discourage in my counseling.

AFFAIRS CAN BRING HAPPINESS AND PLEASURE TO THE PERSON IN AN UNHAPPY, UNFULFILLING MARRIAGE

Whether they provide sexual pleasure, an ego boost, close companionship, or the chance to have new experiences—or perhaps a little of each—affairs have been described as "the ultimate weapon against the marriage blahs." Lovers pursue each other in a separate world, a free-and-easy environment where the troubles that exist at home tend to be closed off and day-to-day irritations are not encountered, at least in the early stages of the relationship.

One forty-six-year-old woman, looking back on her affair, said, "At first, it's a real escape. You're feeling so great that you forget about all the nitty-gritty things that normally bother you at home. My husband and I had so many financial problems, it was an enormous relief just to be with my lover and not have to worry about them or talk about them. I never had to spoil my good time by thinking 'We can't afford this.' " Psychologically, therefore, affairs can be easily rationalized, especially in a culture that endorses an all-out pursuit of one's own pleasure, even if one has to go outside the marriage to find this "happiness."

AN AFFAIR CAN AWAKEN THE MARRIAGE PARTNERS TO THE SERIOUS PROBLEM (OR PROBLEMS) THAT EXIST BETWEEN THEM AND CAN SCARE THEM INTO POSITIVE ACTIONS TO SAVE THE MARRIAGE

Marriage partners often have difficulty in discussing the intangibles in their marriage—such as their feelings of aloneness, anger, or mistrust—until something tangible like an affair forces them out of their complacency. Thoroughly shaken by the discovery of an affair, both partners may then be able to look at and deal with their marriage more honestly and realistically. Admitted one distraught but relieved spouse on the first day of counseling, "Okay, at least my wife and I have a starting point. We can honestly appraise our situation and deal with it accordingly." Before knowing about the affair, he knew something was wrong with the marriage but he could not put his finger on it. When he found out, dialogue and the process of rebuilding their marriage began. Several weeks later he told me, "For the first time in years we are communicating—I mean really talking. I'm ready to accept whatever comes, but I'm pleased that we can at least sit down and get things straight between us."

AN AFFAIR MAY REVITALIZE A MAR-
RIAGE BY PROVIDING A HELPFUL
COMPARISON TO WHAT ONE SPOUSE
CONSIDERS A DULL MARRIAGE

People have told me that they felt there was a certain spark missing in their marriage, so they sampled the field (or just one person), only to find themselves returning to their marriage with a more realistic perspective and new sense of commitment. By falling in love with another person and spending time together in and out of bed, they found that their spouse by comparison looked pretty good—not perfect, but not worth giving up. The irony is that this realization often comes too late to save the marriage. Once the affair has been discovered, one spouse may not take back the other by forgiving and forgetting, and the new-found value in the marital relationship cannot be acted on.

The Cost of Affairs

Although each affair is unique because of the individuals involved, there are common denominators that can help us understand the experience of affairs. I will now take a look at some of the negative results and the impact they can have on the individual involved as well as on the marriage, the children, relatives, and close friends.

LIVING WITH LYING

In my counseling and research over the past ten years, I have found that *the dishonesty that is necessary to sustain an affair is what hurts people the most.* Trying to live with lies, the half-truths, the cover-ups, the subterfuge, and the deceit leads to a disturbing sense of guilt that eats away at one's conscience like a parasite. Although some people are able to live with dishonesty in their lives, most of us have a conscience that is always with us, especially in the bedrooms of other homes or motels.

Matt, the art dealer who had affairs during his two marriages, speaks with authority when he says, "If you're basically honest, it's just too upsetting to lie and to cover. I wanted to be with other women, but I could never really enjoy myself. What got me was not so much the fear of discovery but the constant lying; you don't like yourself when you lie."

A similar perspective is offered by a woman in her early forties looking back on the one affair she had had several years earlier, which broke up her marriage of nearly fifteen years: "You feel so good at first; nothing really bothers you, but then as you get more involved, you have to start lying to your husband and thinking of cover-ups. Sooner or later, it catches up to you. Then comes the guilt."

In recounting his long-simmering affair with his secretary, a New York banker told me, "The pressure during the whole time was incredible. You know what I mean—keeping it going with the lies, the cover-ups. Always the questions from my wife. . . . 'Where were you? What were you doing?' . . . and having a good cover one week, but a week later forgetting which excuse I'd used or getting my excuses confused."

Most men and women believe themselves to be basically

honest and trustworthy, but affairs by their very nature have a strong tendency to undermine that perception. Lamented a woman in her early thirties whose affair destroyed her marriage, "I don't know if I can ever trust myself again because of all the lying I have done."

FEELINGS OF GUILT

Time is a great healer, but often the lying and dishonesty that accompany an affair produce a profound sense of guilt that is not easily overcome. Affairs are always a mixture of pleasure and pain, as we noted earlier, but too often the pleasure is forgotten or fades into the past, and a person is left with the psychological scars. I once counseled a woman who was caught in this classic ambivalence. Married and the mother of a teenage son, she admitted that she had been frigid for most of her marriage until a brief affair with a younger man freed her sexually. "I wanted good sex and I went after it," she exclaimed, "yet I know it was wrong. I was committing adultery and I knew it was immoral." In her mind, "the sneaking, cheating part of the affair was dirty and the guilt was terrible," but she also admitted that it was a good experience for her sexually. "For the first time in my life I felt fulfilled, needed. He made me feel beautiful, and that was something I had never felt before." In this woman's case, the pleasure was fleeting, the pain everlasting—at least until she can resolve the feelings of guilt for what she did.

Guilt manifests itself in another dramatic fashion, as expressed by a woman who had been married twenty-six years before falling in love with a fellow worker. "As the affair blossomed and I began to contemplate a divorce— there was no other solution—I had terrible guilt feelings not only about the affair and what I was doing behind my husband's back, but because I knew I was going to hurt someone I still respected, who really did not deserve it. It would have been much easier to accept my behavior if I had felt my husband had it coming to him, if he had neglected

me or beaten me or chased other women. But he was a
decent, honest guy and everybody liked him. *I* liked him,
too, but I didn't *love* him anymore, and I couldn't stay
married to him."

AVOIDANCE OF MARRIAGE PROBLEMS

An affair is often an escape from the problems that need
careful attention. We are a nation of rug-lifters, preferring
to avoid or gloss over important problems, and this is reflected by the marriage partner who puts his or her troubled
marriage on hold while having a blissful affair. One example
is the husband who kids himself into believing that a long-
term affair or a series of sexually exciting encounters can
justify the continuation of his dull, unrewarding marriage.
If he has an affair going on the side he can then muddle
through with his wife and keep the marriage afloat—"for
the kids' sake"—because of that pleasurable escape he has
with his lover; he may even argue that these escapes are the
only thing holding the marriage together. So why work on
the marriage?

As Los Angeles psychiatrist Dr. Robert Iverson points
out, "If people are really trying to make their marriage work,
affairs for the most part are detrimental. What happens is that
the motivation to make the marriage work gets shot to hell,
because solutions to marriage problems are found in someone
else. It's very tough to work out marital difficulties when
people are off having a roll in the hay with another person,
where none of the regular problems are involved."

THE UNINVOLVED SPOUSE SUFFERS
BY COMPARISON

Not only are marital problems avoided when people
enter into an affair, but the uninvolved spouse is often going
to suffer by comparison. *This adds yet another stumbling
block to reconciliation within the marriage.* A typical example was provided in a letter I received from a woman, who

noted: "A friend, through her own boredom, allowed herself to be conned into an affair. This was very destructive to her attitude toward her husband, who became the scapegoat while she spent hours with Prince Charming." The attractive qualities of a new, exciting lover are easily magnified and glorified when compared with the familiar faults of the spouse back home, and a preoccupation with these differences is common.

When a person has that "in-love" feeling during an affair, he or she obviously finds it difficult to return home with warm, close feelings for the spouse, let alone give the marriage the work and attention it needs. "My affairs kept me from giving my marriage a chance," said a recently divorced insurance salesman from Chicago. "I kept looking for all the negatives in my wife as a way to justify maintaining an affair."

MANIPULATION OF CLOSE FRIENDS

An often unseen yet treacherous happenstance is that old, trusted friends are drawn into a conspiracy to keep an affair secret from the uninvolved spouse. Approached under the guise of friendship, people are sometimes exploited by those having an affair to the point where they often end up doing things they don't particularly like to do or pretending they don't see behavior they disapprove of. They become co-conspirators among friends—and even family members—by supporting the person having the affair and aiding the clandestine tryst, often to the point where there is a test of loyalties.

Here's one perspective, told to me by a bachelor friend in Los Angeles: "An important business associate—a friend since college—came to town one weekend. He was married, but he had his mistress with him and he wondered if he could stay at my house, safely away from company officials at his hotel. I said sure, be my guest, but after they left I didn't like what I had done. I was very uncomfortable about my duplicity. I really liked my friend's wife and here I was giving active approval to her husband's affair. In trying to be a 'good old guy,' I realized I had let my friend manipulate me."

Eventually, there are also the repercussions that can result when an affair comes to light and the uninvolved spouse learns what has been happening behind his (or her) back—that friends aided and abetted the deceitful spouse while professing friendship to him (or her). This realization can hurt as much as the affair itself.

THE RIPPLE EFFECT

The impact of an affair can rarely be contained in that special world of the two lovers, though they might fool themselves into thinking their relationship is hermetically sealed. Whether discovered or not, *affairs are never as cut-and-dried as they may appear on the surface*; they tend to have a ripple effect much like that of a stone cast into a quiet pond: The ever-increasing concentric circles touch more and more lives, and it may be months or years before one realizes just how wide the circles have expanded. This is another important reason we must examine the whole story whenever possible.

Children are invariably victims of a parent's infidelity, for not only do they receive less attention from the parent caught up in the affair, they must live amidst the vindictive anger that surfaces when the affair comes to light. I was involved in a situation where the wife was in such a rage about her husband's affair that her teenage son had to call me and ask that I come over and try to help calm her down. The father wasn't there when I arrived, but when he came in the door the mother began screaming at him in front of the boy and me. "That woman you think you love is nothing but a whore, a cheap sonofabitch!" was just one of her brutal comments. I have since reflected on the psychological scars that will surely be left on the boy and what he is going to think when he is married one day. Will he play back that morning forever and wonder "Is my wife being faithful to me? Is infidelity a part of every marriage?" A similar perspective was expressed by a fourteen-year-old girl who, while baby-sitting for a family in the neighborhood, knew that the husband was having an affair. "One night he came home drunk and even tried to put some moves on me," she said. "If that's what marriage is about, count me out."

A thirty-four-year-old woman in my parish, whose father had had an affair when she was seven, still hasn't reconciled what he did. Everything was still fresh in her mind as she told me with sadness, "I couldn't go to my dad's house after he left my mother without feeling dirty. My mom had told me, 'Your dad left four children at home, and this other woman left two—just so they could live together. How selfish can you be? They did a filthy thing.' I remember that I couldn't even eat my dad's girl friend's cooking because I felt I was being poisoned. I couldn't get out of their house fast enough. I wouldn't even spend holidays with my dad until my husband began to open up communication again. Everything my dad did, I felt, was tainted."

Affairs can also damage wonderful friendships. I was having lunch with a friend and I happened to ask how his business was going. "I think I'm going to have to get out," he said. "My partner is having an affair—the head-over-heels kind—and he's so drained and preoccupied that he's not pulling his weight at work. We're really close friends, but I'm going to go broke trying to cover for him. Besides, his wife is also a good friend and I can't live with myself, knowing what she doesn't know. So I've told him he either has to drop the other woman or I'm going to sell out, and if I have to sell, that will be the end of our friendship. This has been going on for six months and I'm compromised all the time. I've had enough."

Although there are many factors leading to a divorce, when an affair is the most visible, precipitating factor the guilty spouse may not realize until years later just what the

affair brought about. A typical insight is provided by a
woman who reflected on her own affair, which five years
earlier had led to the end of her eighteen-year marriage: "It
still bothers me to think of all the people I hurt by leaving
Wayne for Tony. Not just my close relatives, who all thought
Wayne was a great guy, but cousins and friends of the family
and the people we knew as a married couple whom we may
never see again. What I did left a void in their lives, and a
void in my life."

NOBODY WILL EVER KNOW

I hope that what I've discussed to this point will bring
a clearer perspective to that common rationalization for
having an affair: "If no one knows, who cares? Who's going
to get hurt? If my spouse doesn't know, nobody's going to
get hurt." That may seem to be true, but the fact remains—
you know. Thus, it is imperative to ask yourself, "What is
this affair doing to me? How is it affecting my behavior with
my spouse, my children, my friends, my business or working
associates?" True, you may be the only one who knows (and
usually that assumption is false anyway), but that *one* person
is critically important.

A woman I respect greatly for her honesty in dealing
with her affair told me, "Peter, the idea that I was infatuated
with someone else still bothers me; it hurt me in many ways,
and even though it was seven years ago, I am just getting
back to normal." She was the only one who knew of her
affair; she never told even her best friends, and yet she is
the first to admit that there is no such thing as no one being
hurt by an affair—she was, and that hurt was the deepest.

AFFAIRS DRAIN ENERGY

When two people are caught up in an affair and en-
meshed in the power of Eros, it is usually full-steam ahead
and the world be damned—spouse, family, job, friends, and

society. Maintaining an affair drains one's energy, and there is no way you can keep the affair from negatively affecting the way you relate to your spouse, the time and energy you have for your children, and your ability to function effectively at your job. You have to draw back someplace (if not physically, then emotionally), and usually it is all the phases of your life that suffer.

A lawyer who came to me for counseling started out by acclaiming the virtues of his affair, which was still undetected by his wife after nearly a year and a half. But as we began to probe he admitted that his once-thriving law practice was suffering because his affair was consuming too much energy and concentration. "I'm spending far less time thinking about my clients and much more time scheming how to maintain my relationship with Sally without my wife finding out. I'm at the point where someone or something has just got to go; I can't keep it all up in the air. The mental gymnastics are just too damn exhausting."

IF ALL ELSE FAILS . . .

If all my arguments against affairs have failed to dampen your adulterous spirit, consider these deterrents—the stuff of soap operas and real life:

- The possibility of contracting a venereal disease.
- The risk of losing your job if an intra-office affair comes to light.
- The potential physical retaliation by an irate spouse.
- The trauma of divorce, emotionally and financially. A lawyer friend suggests that men especially should consider what it could mean to them financially. "An affair is an expensive ego trip if it results in a divorce," he pointed out. "One half of a husband's assets will disappear, if not more. So the husband contemplating an affair should ask himself: 'What am I worth, financially—and with half of it gone, how happy will I be?'"

Finally, hard as you might try to camouflage your affair, it could pay to visualize yourself getting caught and the effect this would have on your spouse, your marriage, and your own sense of personal ethics. Said a twice-married counselor, "Something I will carry with me forever is the pain of sitting in a divorce court and listening, in thirty seconds, to the dissolution of twenty years of marriage."

Affairs are never a laughing matter, but in visualizing what could happen in your own affair, try to keep in mind this story that came out of the London *Times* several years ago.

Wedged into a tiny sports car, two secret lovers were having a midnight tryst when the near-naked man was suddenly immobilized by a slipped disc, trapping his woman companion beneath him. The desperate woman tried to summon help by honking the horn with her foot. A doctor, ambulancemen, firemen, and a group of interested passersby quickly surrounded the couple's car in Regents Park. To free the couple, firemen had to cut away the car frame whereupon the distraught woman, helped out of the car and into a coat, sobbed, "How am I going to explain to my husband what has happened to his car?"

CHAPTER 5

Society's Influence on Affairs

Surveys tell us that the vast majority of people approaching marriage disapprove of extramarital affairs. My premarriage counseling, which consists of at least four hours of dialogue with each couple, certainly affirms the fact that when they get married people make a commitment that precludes any extramarital sexual relationship. Sexual fidelity is tacitly, if not explicitly, perceived as a valuable goal for marriage.

Yet at the same time, researchers also have statistics showing that *one half* of the married population will eventually have one or more affairs. The Kinsey people estimate today that roughly 60 percent of all married men and 35 percent of all married women are sexually unfaithful during their marriage. A 1978 *Redbook* survey of 100,000 women found that 42 percent of the working women and 27 percent of the nonworking women who responded admitted to having had an affair. Many marriage counselors state that a "significant majority" of their clients cite infidelity as a precipitating factor in their marital breakdown. Psychiatrists, psychologists, and other people-helpers deal with the issue as a regular part of their work. The Reverend Stan Ramsey of Emmanuel Church in Alexandria, Virginia, typifies the response of clergymen throughout the United States who have written to me about how often they address the subject as counselors or listeners:

"My church serves a relatively stable community in a rather conservative environment where one would suspect little hanky-panky. However, in thinking back over the pastoral counseling that I have done, it is appalling how many people have reported extramarital affairs as part of their problem. In the past year, I have seen more of this than in the previous five years put together.''

Obviously there are many factors chipping away at the wedding-day promise to remain faithful. Over a period of years, situations within the marriage itself and influences outside the marriage increase the possibility of an affair. In the next chapter, I will explore the major reasons people drift—or plunge—into an affair, but first I feel it is important to explore the contemporary social trends that influence extramarital behavior. Today's cultural climate seems to encourage the widely held belief that despite the pledge of fidelity, affairs may in fact provide an experience that is good for you and your marriage. To successfully prevent affairs, I feel it is imperative to be aware of these trends and influences, which are becoming so deeply ingrained as a way of life in the United States.

Pleasure Today, Not Tomorrow

One of the most dramatic cultural influences affecting us is the feeling that we are "owed" an exciting existence. The Protestant work ethic is being replaced by the play ethic, with advertising slogans urging us to live life with gusto because we only go around once. The do-your-own-thing philosophy of the 1960s spawned the "me generation," which has in turn yielded a prevailing social attitude that whatever is fun, thrilling, entertaining, or stimulating is worthy of being pursued; *immediate gratification and pleasure have become prime motivations for life itself.* This attitude is typified by the idea "I want my pleasure now because I've been told I can fly now and pay later," and this is exactly what many people are doing. One young man in his early thirties, whose earning power has enabled him to acquire such expensive toys as a camper and a sail boat, admitted to me very matter-of-factly: "I work so I can play."

My experience has shown that this attitude has spilled over into marriage. Many people who have the pursuit of pleasure as their ultimate goal in life see affairs as a promised elixir: the escapes to romantic getaways, a lively and loving companion, a fresh new body, and the chance to break away from a mundane pattern of life that demands work to bring it alive. All this is remarkably appealing to most of us, especially to those of us who want pleasure today, not tomorrow.

Instead of working hard to solve marriage difficulties, many individuals seek instant solutions. Their theme might be "Hurry up with the excitement. If we can't solve the boredom or blues in our marriage today, I'll find someone to make me happy tonight." We constantly hear the familiar complaint "I'm not going to live like this forever. Life is too short, and while I'm young I'm going to have some fun."

Sexual Permissiveness

Even if our religious beliefs are traditional and our moral standards impeccable, we all live in a permissive, sexually explicit society that is continually influencing our marital behavior. No longer is human sexuality a taboo subject. We can take courses on sex in college, at the local adult evening school, and in some churches. Theologians write candidly about sex, doctors serve on panels that discuss the subject in detail, and radio and television talk shows hold open forums on this favorite subject. From the standpoint that all of this honest, revealing talk is helping us to better understand and improve our sexuality, I rejoice. *Paradoxically, however, our openness about sexual matters has created a more hospitable climate for affairs to develop and thrive.*

Sexual stimuli have become part of our daily existence to an extraordinary degree. Everywhere we turn and from every conceivable source we are barraged with visual and written imagery on all aspects of our sexual nature. Television airs blatantly sexual programs every night of the week—and all day long, once the kids are off at school. The advertising industry tends to sell sex as much as the product, whether it is a perfume ad in *Vogue* or *Harper's Bazaar*, a jeans commercial on television, an actress selling cigars or new cars, or a model on a billboard hawking suntan lotions or a hotel in Las Vegas. Our culture is also very fashion conscious, with men and women alike dressing in casually seductive clothing designed to make them more appealing. These changes, which have occurred during the past ten or fifteen years, have been major, and many people have had difficulty adjusting to them. As one forty-four-year-old business executive told me: "It's tough as hell to handle all these braless young women in the office with their sexy clothes. They didn't tell me about this at Harvard Business School, but it's one of the toughest parts of the job."

Our permissive society has also led to the tendency to wink at the presumed extramarital behavior of some of our public figures—from Adam Clayton Powell to Wayne Hays to presidential candidates, not to mention former presidents. In fact, we have reached the point where we almost expect illicit sexual behavior from people in certain segments of our society—such as ball players, politicians, movie stars, and entertainers. And when we learn about affairs among these personalities, we simply shrug our shoulders and say "What do you expect?" The next step is to exclaim "See, everyone is doing it, so why not me?"

The pervasiveness of sexual stimuli and the general sense of sexual permissiveness have given affairs a veneer of respectability—and something many of us want to pursue. Our tolerance has fostered a new level of acceptance. Although one psychologist argues that since "adultery is being practiced by a large number of devotees, why not permit its reality, and give it an opportunity to succeed or fail?" I feel

that we have already given adultery and affairs plenty of
press—and accolades—and a free run in a society that encourages the pursuit of one's own happiness. Affairs have
been given a remarkably high status in some circles, and
have been blatantly encouraged by such articles as "The
New Kept Women and Their Keepers" in *Los Angeles
Magazine*, which extolled the benefits of having a mistress.

The Language We Use Is a Camouflage

What we once knew only as adultery ("a crime of hein-
ous nature," according to the Bible) now comes to us pack-
aged as a carefree, playful activity: i.e., an affair, a fling, a
liaison, a tryst. Changing language to rationalize behavior is
nothing new, but the introduction of phrases that de-empha-
size the gravity of what happens in an affair—adultery—is
common in our culture today.

The word affair, for example, sounds wonderfully free,
appealing, and romantic. It means "a romantic or amorous
relationship," and it sounds terrific, especially when pro-
nounced with a slight French accent, as in the popular movie
Pardon Mon Affaire. Then, of course, there is nothing serious about "fooling around" or having a fling—no one is
going to get hurt in that kind of fun-filled relationship. A
liaison sounds mysterious and filled with intrigue, while no
one really knows what a tryst means. Just a lot nicer than
adultery, which in contrast sounds cruel and harsh—the original intention. The Latin root is from *adulterium*—adul-
terate: "To make inferior, impure, not genuine; by adding
a poor or improper substance."

But these euphemisms are more than just passive re-
flections of changed moral standards: changing and softening
the language has actively changed our views of affairs, making
them more inviting and less threatening. For even today, to
accuse a person of adultery is to make a serious charge. Peo-

ple tend to respond to "He has committed adultery," differently than they respond to "He had an affair."

In his book *The Extra-Sex Factor*, Dr. Lewis Yablonsky
found that most of the men he interviewed who sought sex
beyond the marriage bed "resented the use of terms like
cheating, infidelity, adultery, and extramarital sex. They
considered these expressions old-fashioned because they pro-
jected moral connotations into behavior they considered to
be guilt free, pleasurable."

Hollywood Hype

The vision we have of affairs comes to us in part as cour-
tesy of what I describe as Hollywood Hype. Movies like *Bob,
Carol, Ted, and Alice; A Touch of Class; Same Time, Next
Year*; and *The Seduction of Joe Tynan*, project an image of
affairs that is enticing and appealing. Commented *New West*
reviewer Stephen Farber after seeing Alan Alda and Ellen
Burstyn in *Same Time, Next Year* act out a common fantasy
by continuing an affair for more than twenty-five years by
meeting just one weekend every year: "We may also wish we
could have this kind of perfect, carefree love affair—sex and
romance divorced from all the responsibilities of full time
relationships." He also noted that "the film slyly glorifies
adultery."

Continuing the Hollywood trend is a recent movie titled
Loving Couples, starring Shirley MacLaine (who herself has
argued that "open infidelity could save a lot of marriages").
Roderick Mann commented on the movie in the *Los Angeles
Times*: "It is a film about a married woman who has an affair
with a younger man. The younger man's girl friend goes to
the married woman's husband for advice and winds up in
bed with him. It's funny stuff." Yet another MacLaine movie,
A Change of Seasons, has her husband, a college professor,
fall in love with one of his students—Bo Derek—which
prompts MacLaine to take a younger lover.

We shouldn't be surprised, of course, that moviemakers keep twisting the eternal triangle for every conceivable plot. This is real life—it happens all the time—and filmmakers like to remind us of that fact. Yet in giving us the Hollywood version of extramarital affairs, they embellish and romanticize what actually happens in most such relationships. In the movies, for instance, the mistress or adulteress is invariably portrayed as a younger, livelier, more appealing woman than the wife. We are almost never shown the average-looking woman with three kids and a husband who takes her for granted, who turns to an equally discontented and ordinary married man in her social circle.

Sex outside marriage also makes for good written copy, with practically every novel and a good number of nonfiction books including an affair or two. Often the affair is the anchor for the plot, as in *The First Lady*, a recent novel by Ron Nessen, the former presidential press secretary. Here is how the publisher describes the book:

"At the center of the novel is Libby Blair. Famous and wealthy, brilliant and desirable, she is the most celebrated First Lady since Jacqueline Kennedy. She seems to have it all—the long, low limousines, the glittering opening nights, the big celebrities, the tycoons, the power politicians. And yet she is running away. She is leaving her husband to start her new life with her lover—the man who was her husband's oldest and closest friend. . . ."

The "friendship" affair, of course.

Affairs Are Still a Laughing Matter

Although national and local talk-show hosts on television and radio have attempted to provide legitimate, open dialogue about affairs, the subject is for the most part a laughing matter elsewhere. I am frequently reminded of this when people say to me incredulously, "You've got to be kidding. You're writing a book on how to *prevent* affairs?

Why don't you write a best seller about how to have an affair and get away with it?" Meanwhile, television comedians joke about affairs all the time, and we laugh with them. For example, Ronnie Shell told Merv Griffin in jest, "I don't have time to date, I'm too busy committing adultery." The joke doesn't make a lot of sense, but he got a big laugh. Even a family cartoon strip, "Blondie," had the following dialogue between Dagwood and Blondie:

DAGWOOD [*reading his paper*]:   What did you do at your meeting today?

BLONDIE: We discussed current affairs.

DAGWOOD: Which ones?

BLONDIE: Mostly Vera's and Edith's.

Affairs get the same laughing treatment alcohol used to get on television when Ruth Buzzi and Dean Martin portrayed two hilariously funny drunks at a bar. Today, with our raised consciousness about the havoc alcohol can bring to our homes, families, and jobs, I am sure our perception of those skits would be dramatically different. *Contributing to our easy acceptance of affairs is the plain fact that we no longer take them seriously enough.*

Looking the Other Way

An overlooked and underrated contributor to the growth of affairs is our complacency about them and our easy acceptance of them within our own close circle of friends. When we are asked to accept a friend's affair, we are being asked to condone behavior that we know can be destructive to the friend and to his or her family. I feel we should accept a friend under these circumstances, because friendship means forgiveness, acceptance, and understanding. However, by turning our eyes from something we personally disapprove of we fail to help this friend. When we let our feelings and beliefs stay hidden, our silence implicitly approves the illicit behavior. In such a situation, we have a right to share our

feelings when a good friend—someone we like and respect—
is caught in the web of an affair.

The Reverend James Sell, a licensed marriage and family
counselor in West Virginia, told me: "My wife and I have
friends who are having affairs, but we don't put them down;
they will remain a part of our social group or congregation.
Yet perhaps we are part of the problem by this easy acceptance
of their behavior. We make it okay in many ways for a person
to get away with an affair. Sometimes we offer tacit approval
by telling an older male friend, 'You old fox you, you sly rascal
you—I don't blame you. If I were in your shoes . . .' and so
on."

The Disposable Mentality

We are all aware that we live in a society where it is
getting increasingly easy to throw something away rather than
save it, wash it, or recycle it. We now have throw-away diapers,
bottles, cans, furniture, and clothing, and I feel many of us are
gradually moving toward a similar discarding of personal
relationships. The disposable mentality has invaded the
sanctity of marriage, and many people today are subscribing
to the motto "If this marriage doesn't work out, I'll dispose
of my spouse and find another one." An attitude like this also
leads people into affairs with a so-what posture: "What do I
have to lose anyway? If I get caught and my spouse leaves me,
big deal—she isn't that important to me anymore."

This devaluing of people and relationships is a disturbing development and is one of the most important reasons I
place such an emphasis on affair prevention. Far too often,
the disposable mentality that accompanies an affair is an
indication of the growing disregard for the worth of another
human being.

My good friend, Marion Baker, whose wisdom transcends
her sixty years, put this idea in perspective when she told me:
"Peter, it is easy to think of reasons and to find reasons to end

a marriage. The hard thing is to find reasons to improve your marriage and to tell yourself that you're not going to throw away what you already have."

The Image We Have Given Affairs

All the elements I have talked about in this chapter have helped create an image of affairs that makes them something we want. Affairs offer the promise of a good time, a lot of laughs, comfortable sex, and an escape from all the problems at home. In fact, if advertising executives could sell affairs on television, they would have a field day appealing to our fantasies. They would show happy, carefree lovers leaving their troubled marriages behind to share the joy and excitement of a wind-blown drive up the Pacific Coast Highway toward an overnight rendezvous in Santa Barbara or Morro Bay. Or these lovers would be holding hands strolling down the beach at Waikiki at sunset, with gulls circling overhead and waves crashing to the beach. Or they would be partaking of romantic night spots with softly lit, beautiful entertainers in the background, the lovers dipping their skewers of beef into fondue while rubbing their feet together under the table. Or they would be flying into Carmel or Las Vegas or the Adirondacks or Cape Cod for the weekend—or checking into a snug Vermont inn. And of course the woman would be stylish and sexy, the man a handsome, successful executive.

Perhaps one day we will even see a notice in the want ads of newspapers and magazines like the following:

"Happy, carefree lovers, leaving their marriages of eleven and fourteen years behind, seek a private cabin, cottage, or home on the beach with a view of the sunset. Four-to-eight-month lease. Convertible wanted, telephone not necessary. Access to a tennis court and Jacuzzi preferable. Box 22, Omaha, Nebraska."

CHAPTER 6

The Whys of Affairs

Rarely is an affair caused solely by one condition in the marriage. Infidelity tends to result from a combination of factors and is usually a culmination of what has been taking place in the marriage over a period of time, what went on in the person's life before the marriage, and external factors that affect the marital relationship. This chapter will isolate and illuminate some of the major factors that precipitate affairs, thus providing important clues and patterns to watch for and avoid in your own marriage.

Trying to accurately assess why someone has an affair is a complicated process. The reasons may seem obvious on the surface, but they might also arise out of deep psychological factors that often are not known or discovered for many years, if ever, even through therapy. I have found during my counseling that most people who have affairs do not need intense psychotherapy. Certainly not those who have contemplated having an affair but have not actually done it.

Granted, some people are by nature not monogamous: they cannot maintain deep relationships for any length of time; some will always destroy personal agreements or contracts; and some, because of long-term mental stress or problems, can never adequately commit themselves to a marital union based on fidelity. Since I don't presume to be a psychiatrist, I will try to avoid probing into the deep psychological reasons people have affairs.

I will instead focus on fairly clear manifestations of marital and personal disharmony that lead to affairs. I feel strongly that the reasons given here will apply to the majority of us who have basically "normal" marriages and personalities and who have a sense of right and wrong in personal relationships. I advocate that you know the basic *whys* of extramarital behavior as an aid in prevention, while being aware that what I am presenting here is simply one part of the picture.

The Sexual Reasons for Affairs

SEXUAL FRUSTRATION

Sexual frustration is inevitably discussed when I counsel people about affairs, whether it stems from too little sex, insensitive sex, or unimaginative sex in the marriage. Societal influences have led us to believe that we all should be enjoying—or at least striving for—a better sex life and that *if our spouse doesn't offer this, then an affair will.* We are constantly reminded that every marriage must have two sexually compatible and happy people. Yet until recently, men have been much more direct than women about determining their need for an affair by how much sex they have with their wife. Many married men judge their sex life by how many notches they cut on the bed post each week and are more apt to play the sexual numbers game than women. They will often admit, in the privacy of my office, "I need to get laid more." Women, on the contrary, are less inclined to use such direct language (though some do), primarily because their needs are defined as more than purely sexual. But as we move into the 1980s, women are feeling increasingly comfortable about expressing their sexual frustration and are trying to openly discuss what that means in their marriage. A typical example of this new openness is the woman who recently expressed displeasure that her husband rarely initiated lovemaking anymore. "I'm horny as hell," she told me, "and all he wants to do is watch the Lakers on TV."

In the past, it was common practice for men to seek out

an extramarital partner if their sex life was unsatisfactory at home (and for some, even when it *was* good at home). Today, married women are much more willing to articulate their own sexual needs directly—if not to their husbands, then to a counselor, or by turning to an affair. The Reverend Bob Iles, a sexual therapist and counselor in Los Angeles, states that "times are giving women freedom to initiate sexual liaisons for their own sake; they just aren't that passive anymore." Women are admitting the same sexual feelings that were once presumed to be the exclusive right of men. In her book *Playing Around*, Linda Wolfe says that "a number of women felt quite strongly that they had taken lovers because at some point in their thirties they had undergone a psychological change that altered their sexual needs. One cluster of these women felt that the sex they had had in their early years of marriage while good was no longer adequate to their present needs; another felt that the sex in their marriage had never been good, but prior to their thirties had not presented a problem."

Sexual frustration, however it is defined by the partner, is a major factor in causing affairs. Yet it is hard to quantify sexual frustration, because what may be frustrating for some marriage partners may be bliss for others. Nevertheless, here are a few examples of frustrating sexual situations that have contributed to an affair's beginning.

- A forty-one-year-old woman, married seventeen years to a traveling salesman, became increasingly frustrated at his absence of one to two weeks every month. "I care for my husband and I want to make things right," she said, "but I can't go on like this. I have to reduce my stress somewhere. I need a sexual release, so I'm going to have an affair."
- A twenty-seven-year-old woman whose impatient and insensitive husband was concerned solely with his own sexual pleasure. They had frequent sex, but he ap-

proached each lovemaking session with a "wham bam, thank you ma'am" attitude. She was seldom gratified by his perfunctory manner, and her frustration led to an affair with a writer who took time to please her.

- A man whose wife requested no sex during either of her pregnancies, which came only thirteen months apart. She declared that sex, besides being uncomfortable, was repugnant to her when she was pregnant. At the beginning of her second pregnancy he began to seek quick-fix sexual relations, telling me later, "Nine months again without sex was something I couldn't bear."

- A father of two teenage children began to seek other women because his wife feared becoming pregnant. She was fearful of the pill's effects, uncomfortable with an IUD and a diaphragm, and suspect of condoms. She could not accept her husband sexually because she did not want another child, yet she held back from becoming sterilized or having her husband get a vasectomy. They said they loved each other, but his frustration grew into an obsession, and he began having sex with women he knew were "safe."

SEXUAL BOREDOM

One of the obvious attractions of an affair is the prospect of better sex, more frequent sex, or different sex. The image is a tantalizing alternative to what may exist in the marriage bedroom when a couple has slipped into the same approach to sex week after week, year after year. States Dr. Raymond Babineau, professor of psychiatry at Rochester University: "Sexual familiarity can all too easily lead to boredom. When partners have experienced each other sexually thousands of times and have seen each other naked, ill, discouraged, and angry, they are in a far different situation than partners enthralled with the novelty of an affair." Thus, a sexual relationship that is dull and unrewarding to one or both participants can motivate them to seek greener pastures elsewhere, for *the attraction of routine sex pales when compared with the glamour of extramarital sex.*

People seek an extramarital partner not just to sample a fresh, new, unexplored body, but because an affair offers them the prospect of sexual experimentation and variety. This rationale was offered by a stockbroker who had been married twenty-five years, but who had had a series of affairs with younger women in their twenties and thirties. "Why?" I asked him. "It's fun," he replied, "and I like firm bodies. But what I like best is that younger women today are freer and more willing to experiment. My wife has never gone for oral sex or different positions. But a younger woman, if she hasn't tried something sexually, she's willing to give it a try."

The sexually frustrated often seek those who are willing to try something or someone new. The concept of "anything goes" seems to have become the ideal, just as long as no one is hurt. Younger people tend to be much more amenable to that philosophy, with fewer inhibitions.

SEXUAL CURIOSITY

After years of remaining faithful to their spouses, some people suddenly have an affair because of curiosity at what they presume they have missed. This is especially true of those who had limited sexual experiences before marriage and whose desire is heightened by the open, sexual nature of our society today. Our natural curiosity fosters a feeling expressed by a banker who was contemplating an affair: "I married while I was in college, and for twenty-one years have led a respectable married life. But my kids are off at school now, and damn it, I want to know what it's like with another woman." Women, too, have expressed this same kind of longing—to know what it's like to be held and seduced by another man.

Edward's attitude represents that of a particular generation of men. He is a thirty-nine-year-old advertising executive, a good family man involved with his children, but who is now carrying on a long-term affair with an art director in his office. I asked him what the motivation for his affair was and he said, "I grew up in an era when sex was still repressed; I had to peek around the corner at it. It wasn't available to me, and I wasn't the kind of guy to score easily as I went through high school and college. Then I got married without dating many other women. I finally got into my affair because I felt cheated, that I had missed out on a lot, especially after reading what the kids are up to nowadays. Now I'm getting all the sex I want, and I'm doing something I've always wanted to do. This extramarital-sex deal is something that has always intrigued me, and I don't want to give it up."

THE NEED FOR SEXUAL AFFIRMATION

As the aging process takes it toll and the view in the mirror becomes discouraging, we all need to know that we are still sexually desirable—at least to our spouse. *If this affirmation of our sexual appeal is missing in our marriage, then we may be tempted to have an affair as a way to restore a youthful self-image through the eyes of a new lover.* A lover will usually accept us just the way we are; he or she finds those old familiar parts new and exciting, and appreciation is offered both verbally and nonverbally without hesitation.

For example, Ken's wife had been neglecting him sexually for several years, virtually to the point of rejecting nearly all his overtures unless she was perfectly rested and the atmosphere was just right. He finally responded by turning to a woman in his office. He later told me, "My sexual needs became all important to me, and I was willing to gamble everything by having an affair. My lover has given me a great deal of confidence because she is constantly praising my performance in bed. She even tells her friends about me, and that makes me feel terrific."

Vanity is also at work here, as pointed out by Gail Sheehy in her book *Passages.* She cites an attitude prevalent among many women: "This is my last chance to have a fling before I lose my looks." My friend Frank, who is fifty-one, expressed typical male sentiments when he said, "Affairs at this age among my friends are mostly physical. Men are thinking they're on the downhill side of life and that 'this is it folks—my last chance for erotica!' It's an ego thing for them. They're afraid of growing old, and they want somebody to affirm their outer being. The externals are all important. They're thinking 'She'll look good on my arm.' "

My own opinion is that a lot of this has to do with psychological age—the age people *feel* they are—rather than chronological age. A thirty-two-year-old married man told me, as he tried to justify his affair, "It makes you feel young to go to bed with a girl just out of college." If he thinks thirty-two is old, wait until he hits forty.

ANONYMOUS SEX

"The affair with Carl was nice," began a twenty-seven-year-old housewife, "because I didn't have to be intimate. It was just good, clean, honest sex. Well, I don't know about it's being honest, but it was fun." This desire for sex without emotional attachments propels many people into affairs because of the presumed brevity of the relationship and the ability to walk away at one's whim, without any intended impact on the marriage. The marriage will remain intact—or so one hopes.

That one good romantic fling with the unknown blonde in the T-Bird in *American Graffiti* is an example of a common fantasy. Uncomplicated sex is the dream of many. Perhaps only first names get exchanged over drinks in a hotel bar—rarely addresses or personal histories—and the partners walk away from their liaison with nothing having been given and nothing received except the pleasure of their time in bed.

These "good time Charlie" affair seekers view life as one good time after another and believe that *personal gratification is paramount*. This message gets translated by many seekers to mean: "If you want sex, just go out and look for it, because it's there for the asking." We tend to think of the stereotypical male here; happily married on the surface for all to see, but scheming for another "score," his ego demanding that he go from one sexual experience to another. Yet Joan Rose, a former counselor at UCLA, told me about a woman friend who was "totally sexual" and always on the prowl for other men. "She's totally liberated, and she doesn't want to get emotionally involved, but I don't understand her," said Joan. "She's like the *Playboy* male you read about. A lot of ladies are like her today—they enjoy their husbands, but they have a need for extra relations"—and apparently they go out and get them.

The Need to Feel Appreciated

Most people assume that sexual needs are the major precipitating factor of an affair. Yet my experience over the years and my personal feelings have convinced me that the need to feel appreciated is the number one reason. If I had to isolate the most common rationale or motivation given by people for having an affair, it would be the statement "My husband (or wife) takes me for granted." Whatever our role might be—as parent, breadwinner, or housewife—we want to feel we are valued by our spouse for who we are and for what we do to make the marriage successful and happy. We expect our spouse to tell us—verbally or nonverbally—that we're worthy.

If these necessary ego strokes are lacking in our marriage, and we're made to feel worthless or unwanted, our vulnerability can lead many of us to risk everything for an extramarital lover. This is typified by the twenty-seven-year-old woman who told me, "I warned my husband 'Pay attention to me or else something might happen.' He never changed, so I felt I had nothing to lose by having an affair."

The great appeal of an affair, beyond the sexual aspects, is that it has the potential to reaffirm one's worth. In a marriage that has gone stale and in which few words or acts of appreciation are exchanged, it can be very flattering to know that somebody of the opposite sex finds you interesting and appealing and wants to spend time with you. The Reverend James Sell puts it this way: "We live wanting to be more fulfilled than we are. Society creates within us a sense of disesteem—the idea that we can always 'do a better job' than we're doing, in our work, our marriage, raising kids. All of us are put down one way or the other; no one is immune. That's one reason an extramarital lover is so appealing—he or she builds us up, doesn't see our commonness, doesn't care to dwell on our bad side."

I recently counseled a man who felt he was driven into an affair by a wife who constantly belittled him. It got so bad that he would do something thoughtful like making breakfast for the family on Sunday morning, and his wife would criticize his using butter instead of margarine. He could do nothing right, so he felt no guilt about pursuing a woman who worked in his office. Their relationship was still going strong after six months when I saw him. "I'm having so much fun with someone who appreciates me," he said. "It's not just in bed, but the whole relationship. My wife never compliments me, and I know I will never meet her standards. She never says, 'Hey, I like what you did for me today.' But Susan is always giving me positive feedback. She'll say, 'My, you look handsome tonight.' I really feel great after that. What it boils down to is when I'm around Susan, I feel like I'm Robert Redford."

This basic need for recognition brought a terrific, very moral woman to the brink of an affair with her tennis pro. Connie, a former airline hostess, was married to a lawyer and raising three children when she came to me for advice. "My ego is shot down," she said. "The pro thinks I'm fabulous, and he wants to have an affair. He's always telling me, 'You're the greatest thing going,' but I'm married to a guy who dumps on me." Connie's husband was in his late thirties and the pursuit of personal happiness seemed to be his major goal in life. He drove a BMW, owned a large sail boat, belonged to a country club, and always had his eye out for another fancy new possession. Said Connie, "I get the feeling with my husband that I'm just another piece of his property, like a stewardess or a legal aide at his beck and call. I don't feel I'm important in his life, and I've warned him many times, 'Don't take me for granted—I'm not a standby. I won't be a puppet. If someone makes me feel like a queen, I'll buy the crown.' "

Yet at the same time, Connie treasured her three children, and she didn't want to threaten their stable upbringing by doing something that could destroy the marriage. This left her with frustrating, ambivalent emotions and feelings toward the advances of the attentive, caring tennis pro. A beautiful, sensual woman, she wanted her "strokes," but she also valued her marriage—if not her husband. Eventually her concern for the children prevailed over the fleeting allure of the affair with the pro. But she admitted she didn't know how long she could live with a marriage like this.

The "Ness" Needs

Affairs begin not just for sexual reasons but to satisfy the basic need we all have for *closeness, goodness, kindness, togetherness*—what I call the "ness" needs. When these needs are not met on a regular basis in a marriage, the motivation may be to find a person who will be good to us, touch us, hold us, give us a feeling of closeness. Sexual fulfillment may indeed become an important part of an extramarital relationship, but the "ness" needs are for most men and women I know initially more important.

Sex therapist Bob Iles believes that companionship is a prime motivation when people seek or let themselves become vulnerable to the appeal of an extramarital partner. Companions are close friends who spend time together and continually care for each other's needs in a kind and giving manner. We tend to think of companionship as something we desire when we are widowed at seventy-four and are no longer romantically inclined. However the desire for companionship knows no age limitations; young and old alike share this need.

I know one young woman, a mother of two young boys, who had an affair simply to be close to someone of the opposite sex. Her aggressive, hard-working husband became totally absorbed in his job in the film industry. He had long, irregular hours and was on location much of the time, while she remained tied down at home with her two preschoolers. Her female friends visited with their kids and shared a cup of coffee, but they went home to husbands who were there every evening and on weekends, so she was alone much of the time. Even when her husband was at home, he had little energy for *her* needs, not just sexually but affectionately. Finally, wanting a close male friendship, she pursued a social acquaintance so she could spend time with another adult away from her children and have her "ness" needs met. She did not want to conquer or seduce this friend, but simply have him as a comfortable, intimate companion.

One of the surprising discoveries I've made from my work with men who have had affairs is that the "ness" needs are more important to them then they or I initially realized. Men may not readily admit these needs because it sounds unmasculine to state such concerns, but *I've found that men often have affairs to experience this feeling of closeness to a woman.* Men increasingly demand companionship at a time when their lives are the most hectic and impersonal. By and large, they live and work in unemotional, nonfeeling environments; business and industry are concerned with profit and performance, not personal feelings, and if a man does not have closeness and togetherness at home, he often tries to find it elsewhere.

"An affair offers close companionship," said an executive with IBM. "I'm a touchy-feely guy and I like women. I want simple affection, not just a roll in the sack, and I'm not getting either at home. I have a capacity to give, and I want an outlet." He had an affair with a co-worker, and he had his needs met by this woman for several months. "We enjoyed just spending time together, holding hands and walking around the park, things like that," he said.

The Allure of Eros

We read about the power of Eros in novels, we see it at work in the movies, and we hear Hollywood starlets on talk shows declare, "I'm so much in love now; I'm finally happy." And we ourselves know that overpowering feeling of falling in love. The songwriters Johnny Mercer and Harold Arlen expressed this sensation perfectly when they wrote:

> That old black magic has me in its spell,
> that old black magic that you weave so well.
> Those icy fingers up and down my spine,
> the same old witchcraft when your eyes meet mine.
> The same old tingle that I feel inside,
> and then that elevator starts its ride,
> and down and down I go,
> 'round and 'round I go,
> . . . In a spin,
> loving the spin I'm in,
> under that old black magic called love.*

Terrific, except that such infatuation has either long been absent or has never been felt by some married people. *Seduced by the image of an affair, many of them turn to one because they want to "fall in love" with someone other than their spouse.* Cupid's arrows work, and the pleasant sensation we call romance is a goal for even the coldest fish among us. That feeling of being in love is talked about and portrayed

---

* Copyright © 1942 by Famous Music Corporation. Copyright © renewed 1969 by Famous Music Corporation.

in such buoyant terms that the implication is clear to many married people: your life is incomplete if you haven't experienced being in love. Since affairs are rarely portrayed as anything but "Love, American Style," with Eros reigning supreme, people consciously seek this one spontaneous, emotional, irresistible love relationship that has long been absent from their marriage.

Our image of affairs is that they offer a "young love," taking us back to our teenage years. "I feel like an adolescent," said one woman in her midforties who was in the early stages of an affair. This is appealing, especially to those who feel they missed those emotions while growing up or in their own marriage.

Boredom

If you feel stuck with what you sense is a boring marriage or a boring spouse, *the temptation is to seek a situation that is alive and stimulating—one that offers the promise of new and exciting experiences.* We're talking about the wife at home who is bored by the unvarying pattern of her daily routine or the husband who thinks "My wife is a bore; she doesn't stimulate me anymore." Boredom is a difficult feeling to dislodge and, if allowed to become habitual, will gradually and subtly coax someone out of their marriage—often to someone else, who is "different and dynamic."

A close friend of mine from Boston typifies what many housewives say they feel about their marriage, often around the seventh to tenth year. "There's a whole world out there, and here I am, in my little house, driving car pools, making beds, fixing meals, living in Wellesley Hills. The temptation is to go for that exciting *something* out there." Happily, Susan and her husband, Ted, have dealt openly and honestly with these feelings and have not strayed, but the combination of boredom and restlessness can spell disaster in marriages where there's less willingness to confront disenchantment.

Dr. Roger Gould, the Los Angeles psychiatrist, has pointed out that one strong appeal of an affair is that "it promises to bring some new level of aliveness that cannot presently be negotiated with the spouse." This is what drove Linda into an affair with a fellow college professor. "I had to initiate everything in my marriage," she said. "My husband lived in an 'I-me-mine' world, and it was like pulling teeth to get him off his rear end to go on a little trip. My lover was just the opposite. He was spontaneous, very active, and had a high energy level. I came alive when I was with him." Linda found someone who could "turn her on," and she was no longer content to put up with the boring, unresponsive mate at home.

The Need for Adventure, Mystery, and Intrigue

Most of us are not content to live lives of quiet frustration. Even after we are married, greener pastures beckon us. The allure of a new body coaxes us. We are fascinated by the unknown. We covet variety in our experiences and interpersonal relationships. We appreciate people different from our spouse. All of these instincts and desires are natural and, in a healthy marriage, will be brushed aside or accommodated in a way that benefits the marriage. *Unfortunately, in marriages where the mystery is gone and the pastures have turned brown, an affair is often seen as the salvation—the chance to introduce adventure, mystery, and intrigue into an otherwise mundane existence.* "Living in a rut is the pits and I want out," one woman told me as she contemplated an affair. She was convinced that an extramarital lover would bring new experiences that would raise her energy level and make her heart beat faster.

Linda Wolfe, in her comprehensive book on the affairs of several women, states that she met "women whose marriages were sound and even successful, who bore no grudges toward their husbands, and who acted out of imperative personal

longings for adventure and variety." Affairs are so alluring
that people are often tempted to have one just to know what
everybody is talking about. As one woman said, "Many of
my friends, when they hit thirty, talk about breaking away
for a fling. They have happy marriages, but they just want
to go off for a weekend with a lover and live out the fantasies
—that's all."

Another basic reason affairs are appealing is that you
know you are sampling forbidden fruit and that you might
get caught. A college friend from Brown University, reflecting
on the affairs he had during his marriage, spoke for many
when he said, "You know that you're doing something not
quite honest, not quite truthful, and this makes the experience that much more exciting. It is an adventure that keeps
you on your toes." A similar perspective was offered by a
married woman in her midthirties who compared an affair's
mystique to those teenage years when she parked in a deserted
alley, on a hillside, or at the beach. "When you park, you
know you might get caught," she said, "but you know no one
is going to put you in jail for making out in a car." This
woman had married at nineteen, divorced, and then married
an older man after their affair broke up his marriage. However, her resolve to remain faithful weakened early and she
had several affairs in a two-year period. She gave a simple explanation of why: "The chase is intriguing. That's the interesting part of an affair. There's no challenge with my husband
anymore. I won that game." She added that she felt she had
grown up too fast and that the affairs helped her recapture
the mystery of adolescence.

The book *Advice from an Old Mistress to a Young Wife*
(as told to Michael Drury), which has excellent insights into
the working of marriage and affairs, offers this advice: "A
general goes into battle, an artist paints, men climb Everest
and fling themselves into the sky, become healers and judge
a crime on past knowledge. They have to for that is the
condition of living—men must be bold or die inside. . . .

Marriage produces its own downfall when it tries to prevent boldness and sew up the future and hope and daring in a bag."

Alienation

In his superb book *Sexual Intimacy,* Andrew Greeley states that "men are impelled toward the woman in the elevator, or toward the luscious secretary, and women toward the man at the cocktail party or the broad-shouldered male who sits next to her on the bus precisely because union with this other is a means of overcoming separation and putting the world back together again."

Sadly, many people today feel like outsiders in their own marriage and in their own home. They feel cut off from their spouse, alienated by his or her hostility or indifference, to the point where an affair promises a magical sense of belonging. They may have a physical place they call home, but home is an attitude or a feeling, and that is absent. One man in his early forties, an oil-company executive, told me that he felt more comfortable in his mistress's apartment than in his spacious home overlooking the Pacific.

"Did you ever have a roommate in college?" he asked me. "That's what my wife and I have going. We live in the same house and the same bedroom, but there is simply friendship between us, without much intimacy. I'm paying for my home and I call it home, but it has become an impersonal place for me. I don't feel I belong there and I don't feel wanted. My real home is eight miles away in a high-rise apartment building on the eleventh floor. I'm accepted there by my lover. I don't feel lonely when I'm there. I can throw my clothes on the floor and put my feet up on a table and just relax. I feel more at home being away from home."

Even those married people who surround themselves with many acquaintances and are continually busy with activities and functions sometimes find themselves feeling alone and cut off at the end of the day when their head is on the pillow. If the spouse on the other side of the bed (or in the other bed) makes them feel like an outsider and has become indifferent to their being there, an affair may become very appealing. *Besides connecting emotionally, lovers connect by their physical act of intercourse, which itself can provide a strong feeling of belonging.* Separation is overcome, even if it is only momentary. All of us have a drive to be an intimate part of someone else's life, and we will go to great lengths to overcome the chasm of separation and find a lover.

Erich Fromm speaks of two lonely, alienated people who find each other in a world of aloneness: "If two people who have been strangers, as all of us are at one time, suddenly let the wall between them break down and feel close, feel one, this moment of oneness is one of the most exhilarating, most exciting experiences in life. It is all the more wonderful and miraculous for persons who have been shut off, isolated without love. This miracle of sudden intimacy is often facilitated if it is combined with or initiated by sexual attraction and consummation."

"Stop the World; I Want to Get Off"

An affair may promise deliverance not only to the bored, the unhappy, and the alienated, but to those people who are living frenetic, pressured lives. After we marry and as we begin to raise our children, career, societal, and communal demands increase and begin to weigh heavily on our shoulders. As good parents, we know it is important to be involved in everything from our children's school and extracurricular activities to community and religious organizations. Simultaneously, as we try to juggle these many commitments, we try to meet the needs of our spouse.

Eventually, *all these pressures inside and outside the marriage can push us toward relationships that appear to be totally free of demands, expectations, and responsibilities.* Caught up in a push-pull pattern, we may cry out in frustration, "Stop the world; I want to get off." And off often means with Bob or Carol or Ted or Alice. Like a beckoning siren call, an affair offers an escape from reality, at least initially.

Marital Suicide

There is a petition to God asking "Deliver me, O Lord, from the way of sin and death," which has been twisted today to sound like this: "Deliver me, O Lord, from a deadly marriage into the way of sin." Many people who have had affairs admit that a prime motivation was the realization that the affair, once discovered, would help bring a decisive end to a marriage they didn't want to try to save or that they did not have the strength of conviction to close outright by simply asking for a divorce. Analyzing the results of a survey of unfaithful wives for *McCall's,* Natalie Gittelson writes: "The wives who 'kiss and tell' are almost always those who, consciously or unconsciously, seek to terminate the marriage. The affair, for them, is a way of trying to say goodbye."

Many people who consciously start an affair have made a decision that they have basically given up on their marriage. Well aware of the potential consequences of their actions, they would still rather enjoy the affair and let their marriage take its course. You may tell yourself you don't want to hurt your spouse, but once you commit yourself to another person via an affair, there will probably be damage done because your spouse is likely going to find out about it. Advised one man who was still in the midst of a year-long affair: "Once you have started down the road with an affair, you have made the decision that you are going to get caught eventually. You may never want your spouse to know because you realize the hurt it will cause, but if you are honest with yourself, you just know that some day it will all impact on your marriage." Like so many other people, this man will not bring himself to end the marriage outright, even though he knows this will probably be the result once his wife discovers his extramarital involvement.

Taking this rationale for marital suicide a step further, affairs can also be perceived as offering a "can't lose" situation, emotionally and practically. Not only are the lovers escaping a troubled marriage, they are having a good time on the side. Moreover, the spouse having the affair knows that should it be discovered and a divorce initiated, he or she will have somebody to fall back on for love and support. In essence, the affair can become a balm that is spread over the wounds generated by the trauma of discovery and the possible divorce and can help soothe the transition from marriage to being single.

Affairs may also allow a transference of guilt in some cases. For example, if the wife discovers an affair and demands of her husband that he "get the hell out," he can rationalize his behavior by thinking "She was to blame in the first place for my affair, and now she's kicked me out." Even though he was the one to have the affair, she was the one who wasn't accepting and forgiving. So not only does the husband get out of a marriage that wasn't working well, he can feel blameless at the same time.

Revenge

In many marriages, over a period of time, resentment toward one's spouse can reach a point where an affair is perceived as the only way a spouse can fight back or "get even" for general neglect. Sad but true, *infidelity is often seen as the surest, quickest way to "settle the score" with one's mate*; nothing short of an affair will have the same devastating effect.

Sandy, a housewife who was honestly committed to raising her children and caring for her home, became increasingly resentful of her husband. He would arrive home from work after the kids were fed, scrubbed, and ready for bed, pour himself a drink, and then plop himself down in front of the television, claiming to be too exhausted for anything else, be it conversation or sex. I eventually talked with her husband, but only after Sandy had come to me for counseling—and *after* she had started divorce proceedings.

The husband was unusually candid in admitting that he had become married to his job at the expense of his marriage to Sandy. "I was in business with another fellow," he told me, "and I was working six days a week, ten to twelve hours a day. When I came home I'd be so damn tired I never wanted to go anyplace, and I certainly wasn't much in the mood for sex. I was also a little panicked financially because the business was slowing down and I was running out of money. This has been written before, but if a guy is doing fine financially he's doing fine in bed; if he's not, then he's lousy in bed. At least that was the case with me. So after about a year of this, when it was clear that I wasn't going to ease off at work, I couldn't really blame my wife for cheating on me. I was neglecting her—rejecting her—and she went out and rejected me in the classic way."

This situation is often reversed in many marriages. Men feel similar resentments and react to a bad situation at home by committing adultery. The husband may begin to feel cheated because he senses his wife is caught up in her own world. He may only see the tennis and bridge, the luncheons, shopping trips, telephone conversations, and volunteer activities, and may begin to think she has little time or energy left over to cater to *his* needs.

One husband made it very clear that the revenge motive was the foremost reason he began pursuing other women. He had experienced years of being torn down at home, where he was made to feel like a third class citizen. He felt his wife's friends came first, his three children second, and he third. He succumbed to the temptation of another woman because of this simmering anger at his wife. He said emphatically, "Very few people, if they are honestly in love with their spouse, will step over the line and do something that is as potentially harmful as an affair unless their desire for revenge has reached a certain point—where they can rationalize or justify the damage that occurs. In my marriage, I felt the debt had become large enough to justify my behavior. I also knew that there could be nothing more damaging to my spouse than what I was doing by having the affair."

I clearly heard this man's dilemma, and I felt empathy for him. Deep down in his heart he really loved his wife of fourteen years, but the die was cast and he had too many years of built-up resentment to be able to forgive and forget.

Mirror Behavior

The revenge-resentment pattern leads to affairs in yet another way, through what psychologists term "mirror behavior," but what we may call "what is good for the goose is good for the gander." Said an angry housewife, "My husband has been cheating on me for years, so he can't complain when I go out and mess around." In her mind, she had good and sufficient cause to pursue someone else and was justified in using an affair to strike back at a man who had deceived her.

Another aspect of mirror behavior leading to an affair is illustrated by a very fashionable Kansas City matron whose prominent husband led a visible, highly intense life-style and who had sexually neglected her for several years. I never could understand why because this woman was attractive and desirable. Still, one day she discovered that he had been spending his energy chasing and catching younger women in other towns on his frequent business trips. Her original reaction was to find her own lover just to prove to herself that she was still appealing to men. But once her affair was under way, she rationalized her actions by thinking, "Okay, James [her husband], we're even. You've been playing around for years and now I'm doing the same."

This conscious effort for revenge on the part of a hurting spouse may seem unromantic and manipulative, but it is a normal reaction, especially of someone who has a history of being competitive with his or her spouse. I have recently seen more of this attitude in women. Linda Wolfe states that we "tend to view women's adultery as rising out of reaction rather than self-propulsion." However, in my personal experience many women who have had affairs have often been self-asserting and have no longer accepted the stereotypical role of the quiet, uncomplaining, turn-the-head wife at home. Many other women are obviously determined not to allow the double standard regarding infidelity to be perpetuated. This fact, taken all by itself, helps explain why affairs are more prevalent today and are certainly likely to increase.

As an example, John, a computer salesman, began to take extended business trips with a female employee of the same large corporation. He was attracted to her sexually, and his good looks helped break down her resolve, leading to an illicit romance. John's wife, Debbie, eventually assumed that the late hours and the unusual Saturday meetings signaled an affair, and when she found motel receipts in his favorite sport coat, her suspicions were confirmed. But instead of confronting her husband, she kept quiet and casually but deliberately pursued a neighborhood friend of long standing. He finally gave in to her advances, and they began a very intense love affair. "I'm convinced," Debbie later told me, "that I would never have had the affair just on my own initiative. But my guilt was taken away from me because I was just doing what John was doing. Besides, we couldn't and wouldn't communicate, so we both turned to someone else."

Peer Influence

Having an affair to go along with the crowd is not uncommon among certain segments of our culture today, reflecting an attitude that "everyone is doing it—why not me?"

A young estranged husband in Los Angeles blamed the breakup of his marriage on the fact that his wife was "always listening to two of her damn friends about how miserable they were in their marriages. They were both having affairs, and they didn't have any guilt. Pretty soon my wife began to feel that she was also getting a lousy deal at home, and the next thing I knew she had a lover."

I saw peer pressure working in another way several years ago when I met with a group of friends in Columbus, Ohio, to discuss a new concept in ministry. We worked hard until midafternoon and then adjourned to a downtown athletic club for some exercise and a swim. Afterwards, two of us took a steam bath, joining five distinguished-looking Columbus businessmen who happened to be talking about their extramarital exploits. The braggadocio was impressive, and all but one of these men (and the two of us) bantered back and forth for nearly an hour. The silent partner was caught in a classic "Be one of the guys" situation that is so familiar to men from the time they are teenagers. Perhaps he was unaffected and totally convinced that he didn't have to cheat on his wife to enjoy his marriage, but the impression was clearly given that to be successful in that circle of male friends and to be welcomed in the steam room at lunch, he should be able to contribute war stories about his sexual activity.

Another example of even more direct peer pressure was provided by a caller to the "Phil Donahue Show" during a discussion of extramarital affairs. Said the caller, "I was a businessman who did a lot of traveling in connection with my work, and I feel that infidelity almost goes past the point of temptation when you travel. I had a boss who, for six months, would almost never speak to me when we were out on the road. Yet six months later, when I saw a woman who was an old friend in a hotel at eight o'clock in the morning I hugged her. My boss saw this and he thought it was the greatest thing I'd ever done. We were best friends from then on because I had supposedly been unfaithful to my wife."

"In other words," said Donahue, "he thought you were seeing this woman?"

"Yes, he did."

"And that sort of confirmed to him that you were 'normal' to him?"

"Yeah. He himself had people on the road arrange things for him. But I didn't approve of it. I was finally 'caught' and it was like 'Ah ha, you have fallen into the trap.' "

Timing, Availability, Opportunity

For an affair to take place, availability, timing, and opportunity usually come together. People are available, people are seeking, people have the opportunity, and if the timing is right, watch out—an affair just might happen.

A screenwriter friend suggests that "the greatest deterrent to affairs is the lack of opportunity when you are ready." He was jesting, but in reality he may be right for many people. Friends have told me that "the timing wasn't right," or "I couldn't find someone who wanted me when I was looking," at a vulnerable time in their marriage. The opportunities were not there when everything else was perfect for an affair. However, in our society today, it is rare when opportunity does not knock. Unless we are absolutely blind to what is happening or we consciously choose not to see, *opportunities to have an affair will be available to nearly everyone at some point in the course of the marriage.*

This greater access to willing members of the opposite sex makes it easier for an affair to get under way by helping to break down the resolve we might have. Wherever we turn—at the office, in the teacher's lounge, at cocktail or dinner parties, at class reunions—we discover single, married, or formerly married people at every level of society who are comfortable in making it known that "I am available." For example, in former times the wedding ring was a clear and definite sign that said "Hands off, I'm spoken for." Today, that same ring may actually be a beacon rather than a stop sign. In talking about the unmarried secretary in his office, one businessman related a typical situation in today's business world: "She knows I'm married, but she wants to go out with me anyway."

Though opportunity and availability may be present in a given situation, the timing must still be right. A couple of years ago a young mother and her husband went to their tenth college class reunion, taking along their six-year-old son. While her husband was off attending meetings and lectures, the wife walked around campus with the boy. There she bumped into an old college sweetheart, who was recently divorced. "I saw him and the years disappeared," she said, "and all the people around him disappeared. We spent the rest of the day around campus, exploring familiar old haunts and recalling the good times we had together. I kept thinking, 'How can we sneak off to the Holiday Inn?' but my son was like a chastity belt. He was a blessing and a curse. I was so glad he was there, but I was also annoyed he was there." Valerie had two of the three ingredients going for her— availability and opportunity, but the timing wasn't right.

CHAPTER 7

Setting the Groundwork for Prevention

We have looked at the whys of affairs, the types, the pros, and the cons. All of these insights are necessary for prevention and enable us to now shift to skills that will help individuals and couples improve their marriage while avoiding the extramarital pitfalls along the way.

I first want to develop some important philosophical concepts that are crucial to laying the foundation for a successful marriage and for affair prevention. I will then get into the more practical, day-to-day actions that are needed to make this philosophy work.

Developing a Prevention Mentality

In essence, our goal should be to develop a prevention mentality in marriage: a realistic understanding of infidelity and the danger of waiting to deal with this issue on an after-the-fact basis. I liken this approach to holistic medicine, where people are discovering they can avert ill health through prevention attitudes and a sensible system of taking care of their bodies. Why not apply the same philosophy to our marital relations? We cannot transform all of our attitudes overnight, but we can start to change immediately.

One deceptively simple and generally effective element

84

of the prevention mentality is the power of personal conviction and the will to succeed in marriage.

Asked what makes a good marriage, one psychologist answered: "You must be determined to remain married. There must be an active and conscious effort to keep the marriage going." The "I can and I will" school of marriage therapy, taken alone, often does not work for very long, since the appeal of other men or women can be a great seducer. However, married partners who continually reinforce their positive attitudes about marriage and combine these with other skills will have greater success in maintaining their marriage.

Another aspect of the prevention mentality involves the popular theme of taking responsibility for your own life.

This idea that "I am responsible for my own actions, my own well being, and my happiness" is certainly not a new concept, but it is crucial as you try to sift through the advice coming from people who are eager to tell you how you should be living your life. They have a book they want to sell you, a movie, a new life-style, or ideas about marriage that can easily lead you into an affair *if* you abdicate responsibility for your sexual behavior outside marriage.

Dr. James R. McCormick, a Methodist minister in Los Angeles, preached a sermon about marriage in which he stated: "I refuse to believe that we are helpless victims of forces beyond our control. I believe that we are in charge of our lives, and that if we place a high enough premium upon our marriages and if we are willing to work at them, then we can live together happily."

We laugh at Flip Wilson's marvelous character Geraldine, who is always quick to remind us that her bad behavior was not her fault at all. "The devil made me do it" is her famous escape clause. Unfortunately, many men and women affect this same posture when it comes to their own marital health. Even enlightened people see infidelity in marriage as the fault of someone or something else. "I can't help the situation anymore," claimed an exasperated house-wife in my parish. "I've done everything I can." She went on to describe the night of her first sexual experience with a high school football coach. "We went out to dinner, and then we walked around the marina for a while. I didn't want to go drinking, but he insisted. We ended up back at his place, and then one thing led to another, and the next thing I knew he had my clothes off." Her explanation of why all this happened began with the line "If my husband had just not been out of town . . ." She proceeded to chastise the bottle of Scotch, the moonlight, the music on the stereo, and the "aggressive" young coach. Not once did she assume respon-sibility for her own actions.

The third foundation element of a prevention mentality is to know your life principles.

When you honestly know what is important in your life, then you can say to yourself, "That person is of value to me . . . This relationship matters to me . . . These things are of real and lasting value—and here is why." Knowing what or who is valuable and then actively working to pre-serve these aspects of your life will give you a firm footing in your marriage.

I remember a weekend trip I took with my daughter Jennifer and Bill Mingst and his daughter Missy to the Alisol Ranch in Southern California and the conversation I had with a twenty-eight-year-old carpenter-handyman who was putting wood in our cabin for the evening fire. Howard Williams, a graduate of Humboldt State College, was en-gaged to a nurse from the local hospital. We began to talk about my book because he noticed papers all over the cabin and he was curious. I asked him what he thought about affairs and he said, "This is a rule I have for myself: I would leave my wife if she had an affair, and I wouldn't blame her if she left me if I did the same. She is Catholic and has old-fashioned ideas about sex, so we share the same ideals. I've worked hard with this lady, and I'm not about to lose my respect for myself or for her with a stupid affair."

You may not agree with his life principle, or you may think he is naive or overly dogmatic, but I respect someone who has a standard for personal behavior and is willing to live by it without worrying what someone else is going to think—provided that standard does not harm others or infringe upon their rights.

I have found over the years that people who are willing to ask the big questions in life (What is important to me? Who is of value? Where am I going in my life?) are those who have an easier time asking and answering the less lofty but crucial questions such as Am I working at my marriage? Am I falling in love with someone else? Do I spend quality time with my spouse or kids? What is appropriate marital behavior?

Knowing our life principles may not prevent affairs, but this insight by a psychologist is very accurate: "In order to live in emotional equilibrium, our beliefs and behavior must be in harmony. If we do not conform our behavior to our beliefs, we will adjust our beliefs to accommodate our behavior." If our main reason for living is to achieve power and wealth, we may sacrifice family and friends along the way; if we fall in love with someone other than our spouse, we may disaffirm our belief in the vows of the wedding service. So knowing and stating the principles we live by and committing ourselves to them will give us a greater ability to prevent behavior that we might later regret.

One story that illustrates the importance of this philosophy involves a good friend, whom I will call Marty. He was in his late thirties, highly successful financially, overly committed to a variety of enterprises, and at times floundering through life. His position and power led to golf and tennis games with celebrities and parties at their homes, but he was discovering as he approached forty that the happiness and peace of mind he sought—and thought he deserved—was eluding him. His marriage of fifteen years had gone through ups and downs, and at one point he honestly thought that other women, along with all of his material success, could bring him the contentment he wanted.

We started to talk about this one evening after he came to me for advice about how to extricate himself from a brief affair he was having with a woman at work. I used this opportunity to try to help him realize the risks he was taking with his continuing sexual liaisons, and I urged him to really take stock of his marriage and his family life. I could tell his principles of life were not clearly stated, and thus elusive, which helped make him vulnerable to affairs.

Over the next several months I tried to help him discover the people and things that were of real value to him, but my counsel was relatively ineffectual until Marty and his family went off for a weekend. Upon returning home he called me to exclaim, "Peter, I can't tell you what a great weekend we had. The four of us went out in a canoe for hours together, and we just kept talking. Then we took long walks together and had picnic lunches in the woods. In the evening we just rested in the cabin and played games on the floor or read by the fire. Nothing fancy for three whole days. Now I'm realizing that the simple things with my family are what I value—nothing else is as important as that to me. But, damn it, Peter, why couldn't I see that before?"

Here was a person, like so many other men and women, who had the trappings of success but little real happiness until he finally had the strength to ask the big question: What is of real importance to me? Is it owning a big house, driving an expensive car, having a mistress at my beck and call? "Hey, Peter, here it is in a nutshell," said Marty. "Being with my family is really what I value, and I never realized that what I had was so special until I almost lost it." After that weekend with his family, Marty began to change his behavior so he could line up his beliefs with his behavior. That made it easier to live in peace with himself.

Another example involves Dave, who has had a series of affairs during his twenty-year marriage. When I asked him whether he had any regrets about what he had been doing during these many years, he responded, "I'm threatening a life-style that has a history and a continuity and that was once well-chosen—having a wife and children—for one that is of no ultimate value. I've changed my values just to ease my guilt." His awareness of this has helped him work through his desire to sample every new secretary in the office, and he now wishes that he had taken a tougher moral stance before ever venturing into his first affair. He realizes that by tasting the extramarital experience—and the immediate gratification it brought him in comparison to his marriage—but failing to take stock afterwards he had left himself open to future affairs while gambling his marriage.

Many of us come to that fork in the road at vulnerable times in our marriages. One road beckons with extramarital experiences that have been glamorized on stage, screen, and television. The other road challenges us with the less immediate rewards of working out marital problems. Of course, this second option is a basic life principle stated in our marriage vows, but the conflict that ensues with our human nature as the marriage proceeds is very real. Said one married friend about his long-term lover: "The difficulty for me is that the immediate off-the-shelf item is much more appealing than the prospect of having to go through therapy to make the sexual relationship work with my wife. Sex just doesn't work for us anymore, although it should be so simple by now." One underlying reason can be seen in another statement he made: "Every time my mistress wants to leave me, I have a new resolve to make things work with my wife, but she never leaves me and the old resolve quickly dies."

As we wrestle with contemporary pressures and attitudes about infidelity, my hope is that like the traveler in Robert

Frost's poem "The Road Not Taken" we can all one day exclaim:

> I shall be telling this with a sigh
> Somewhere ages and ages hence:
> Two roads diverged in a wood, and I—
> I took the one less traveled by,
> And that has made all the difference.*

The fourth prevention building block is developing a wedding vocabulary.

If you are like me, you probably have a heck of a time trying to recall what was said at your wedding, and you will most likely nod in agreement with the lady who told me, "I had so many other things on my mind that day, the words just passed me by." But on that special day when you and your spouse stood together to be married, the two of you proclaimed to the world—and to each other—that you would live a life together of love, commitment, and fidelity.

"Rachel, will you have this man to be your husband to live together in the covenant of marriage? Will you love him, comfort him, honor him, and keep him, in sickness and in health, and forsaking all others be faithful to him as long as you both shall live?"

"I, Henry, take you, Rachel, to be my wedded wife; to have and to hold from this day forward, in sickness and in health, to love and to cherish until we are parted by death; this is my solemn vow."

Granted, your wedding vows may have been worded differently, but the sentiment behind the "I do" or "I will" is captured here. Around the time of your wedding and during those early days of being in love with your spouse, words like love, sharing, mutual joy, everlasting commitment, sacrifice,

---

* From *The Poetry of Robert Frost* edited by Edward Connery Lathem. Copyright 1916, © 1969 by Holt, Rinehart and Winston. Copyright 1944 by Robert Frost. Reprinted by permission of Holt, Rinehart and Winston, Publishers.

consistency, and fidelity were hopefully a part of your vocabulary. If these words were not explicitly used, then certainly the spirit was implied. The question is, have you since overlooked those words that were spoken with such fervent belief on your wedding day? And has a *divorce* vocabulary quietly taken over? In many marriages, couples get stuck on words like separation, anger, divorce, boredom, swinging, do your own thing, open marriage—words that are repeated over and over until they come to dominate their conversation and thought. When this happens, acting out those words may not be far behind.

I encourage you to uncover, discuss, and maintain a wedding-day vocabulary in your marriage. This reaffirmation of your wedding vows, a determination to understand what the words mean, and a resolve to live up to the standards implied may sound like a preacher's prescription for marital bliss. Yet hear me out. We are usually known more by what we do than what we say, but the vocabulary we use in our private thoughts and in what we say to our mates helps us formulate who we are going to become and the kind of marriage we are going to have.

Covenant, Fidelity, and Mystery

Premarital counseling is enjoyable for me, a chance to get to know young people better and to learn what they are thinking about prior to marriage, when they are madly in love. During the four or five hours we spend together talking, one thing that impresses me is the deep concern they have for what they are actually going to say in their wedding service. Individual words are very important to them, so it is easy for me to sneak in my emphasis upon three words in particular—words we use infrequently today and that we tend to associate with "religious types," but words that have a lot to do with the ultimate success of a marriage: *covenant, fidelity,* and *mystery*.

By definition, covenant means a pledge or a promise—a formal, solemn, and binding agreement. This idea, as derived from my Judeo-Christian heritage, was illustrated by the relationship established between God and the people of Israel. Even during their periods of worshiping idols and fertility goddesses, God did not abandon His people. We will not always live up to this lofty ideal in marriage, for we are human and fallible, but if we can develop this type of respect for binding personal relationships, we add a powerful ally to our affair-prevention arsenal.

In marriage, a covenantal relationship is an ideal, a goal to be sought. Everything derives from this understanding between husband and wife, sealed with the exchange of rings. We pledge we will work together and exhaust all means to keep the marriage going through times of stress and turbulence. This emphasis on the value of covenant was described in a particularly appealing way by Dr. McCormick in the sermon cited above:

> You've never heard a marriage ceremony in which the minister asks you to love one another as long as you feel like it . . . or as long as everything works out well . . . or as long as your spouse is nice to you too. No, what we ask you to promise is "to love one another for better, for worse, for richer, for poorer, in sickness and in health till death do us part." We've removed all the loopholes. It's an unconditional commitment! And the reason we ask people to make that commitment is not just because it's pretty . . . but because that's the only basis on which marriage has any chance of working.

An inherent virtue of the covenant approach to marriage is the fact that such a philosophy undergirds our way of thinking and may make us far less likely to succumb to the easy appeal and escape promised by an affair. The covenantal model has been a beacon lighting the way for couples throughout the ages, deterring many from pursuing another person during times of crisis in the marriage.

Not too long ago, after finishing two sets of tennis, my

friend Ralph and I took a walk through a nearby park to cool down. No sooner were we away from the courts than he abruptly changed the subject and confided that his marriage was in big trouble but that he and his wife, Barbara, were actively struggling to keep it alive. They were seeing a marriage counselor, yet Ralph was convinced that it was the promise he had made in his wedding ceremony thirteen years earlier that kept him from having an affair with a lady who was willing. His body was willing, his mind was saying yes, but his covenant spirit said no. "Come hell or high water, Barbara and I are going to make this relationship work," he said. "We have invested a lot in each other, and we have three great kids. We're not about to blow it apart unless we have exhausted all resources available to us."

Barbara and Ralph based their marriage on love *and on promise*; shared words that meant something to them and were not easily discounted. Unfortunately, this linking of marriage and covenant is not common today. Instead, marriage is often perceived as a contract, reflected by the attitude "Ah, what the hell—if this marriage stinks I'll just find someone else, get a divorce, and remarry." An attitude like this going into a marriage, or at any point along the way, leaves too much room for escape and too little restraint on having an affair in times of anger, disenchantment, and boredom. Couples with a contract mentality promise to live together until the love runs out.

On several occasions I have been asked to support the line "I will be faithful as long as we both shall love" in the marriage ceremony. I tell the couple that this is an unrealistic statement if they expect their marriage to last and that by saying this they're really not putting much stock in the *promise* of their relationship. "I want you to look at the promise as well as the love," I tell them, "and be realistic about the love. Your naiveté is coloring your feelings. Love alone conquers very little and not for very long." After thinking about what I've told them, the couples have agreed to take out the equivocation from their vows and we proceed from there. I cannot agree to make this kind of statement in the wedding ceremony because I would be supporting the theory that if you no longer feel love for your spouse, then being unfaithful is the logical next step. Perhaps this would be so if love were strictly a feeling, but authentic love is more than just warm, fuzzy feelings—and marital love ebbs and flows during the course of any marriage.

Although we should bind ourselves in marriage with a promise of covenant, there is a kind of contract that may be helpful in our marriage—one that guides our day-to-day living. Julie and Paul had a contract that defined how they went about the business of living their marriage, and it was open to continual reappraisal and renegotiation. For example, they recognized that after thirteen years of marriage they had a mutually unrewarding sexual relationship—much too infrequent for Paul, not enough tenderness and intimacy for Julie. Rather than dissolve the covenant, or have an affair—which would dissolve that vow of covenant in their eyes—they dissolved the old unspoken contract which declared that Julie, as a dutiful wife, was to serve Paul in bed. Her needs were not important in the old contract, but were clearly spelled out in the new contract. This renegotiation enabled them to clear one crucial hurdle toward reawakening a dying marriage.

As I advise the couples I marry, the practice of contracting day-to-day living does not just happen; it is an art that needs practice and refining to keep a marriage alive and thriving. Most marriages will not withstand the test of time—and other men and women—without contract and covenant being linked and continually reviewed.

The second word to consider is fidelity. We tend to think of fidelity as a code of sexual conduct in marriage that precludes having sex with anyone other than our spouse. To many it is an archaic word, rarely heard or used.

Others tend to view it from the negative side—infidelity—
and thus the positive value of the word loses its significance.
Yet to pledge yourself to fidelity (to say "I pledge my faithfulness") does not imply only sexual exclusivity but a commitment to remain devoted to one's duty, vows, and
obligations.

Father John Powell, in a superb little book titled
Unconditional Love, gives us this gem about fidelity: "Unless
you give your word and your promise of fidelity to another,
there can be no real trust and consequently no authentic
relationship or secure framework in which two people can
grow." Fidelity may be an old-fashioned word, but it reflects
a very contemporary value of human behavior: the ability
and willingness of both partners to remain loyal, to keep
their promises, to follow through, and to honor their word.
If they value fidelity, it develops into a permanent attitude
that colors their entire approach to life together.

In marriage, we affirm a type of faithfulness that is ideally
without limitations, restrictions, or qualifications. It is not
fleeting or transitory, nor dangled as a reward, where one
spouse says "Honey, I will remain loyal and faithful to you
just as long as you do this and you don't do that." This kind
of sentiment permeates too many marriages, leaving the
options open when they shouldn't be. The Reverend Jo
Tartt, of Washington, D.C., told me about a wedding service
he performed in which he allowed the couple to vow "We
agree to promise that we will cleave mostly unto each other."
In retrospect, Jo realized that he had participated in their
equivocation; he also wished he had followed his gut feeling,
which told him the marriage was doomed from the outset.
He was right—it lasted barely two years.

Although I strive to preserve the use of the word fidelity
in our culture I do not look askance at weddings in which
the word is not even mentioned. However, I feel that as we
respect each other's word, we respect each other. *Our actions*

*follow our words, and the word fidelity and the action it
implies belong in every home.*

Something else belongs in every marriage—mystery.
Almost without fail, people with a thriving marriage talk
about its ability to keep unfolding in new and mysterious
ways, while becoming something better and more fulfilling in
the process. This philosophy is articulated by Carl Rogers,
the eminent psychologist who has compared the best of
partnerships to a flowing stream. "You are not sure where
the stream is going, and the current may take you in a variety
of directions," he said, "but you are traveling it together and
you aren't in one static place because the stream—like a marriage—is a process."

Mystery in the marriage is not something you can insert
on cue as the need arises. Rather, mystery evolves as you
keep yourself open to the possibilities of newness in the
marriage through your own personal growth. Surprise your
spouse with new interests or hobbies that make you more
alive and more interesting, while encouraging his or her own
pursuits—taking extension courses at a nearby university,
reading books in a special area of interest, researching places
to travel, getting involved in church and community activities, and so on. As my ninety-year-old grandmother used to
tell me, "Peter, each year with your grandfather was as good
as the one before, and you know why? We never stopped
getting to know each other better; there was always something more to learn—even when he was eighty-three."

Each of us is a unique creation of God, continually
changing in manifold and not always logical ways. Similarly,
a marriage is a living organism in which two growing,
changing people choose to go through life together. And part
of what keeps the marriage vital is that it keeps flowing and
it doesn't stagnate. When I hear people declare that the
spark has left their marriage or that they no longer get a lift
out of being with their spouse, I sense that mystery is missing

from the relationship; the process of unfolding has stopped and predictability and sameness have settled in.

Covenant, fidelity, and mystery may not be household words, but they will remain cornerstones of all strong human relationships. They are words for affair prevention in the 1980s and beyond.

CHAPTER 8

Extramarital Behavior

Very few of us go through our married lives relating only to our spouse, family members, and a few close friends of the same sex. We are social animals, and we interact with potential lovers all the time—on the job, around the neighborhood, in community activities, in social situations, and while traveling. I strongly favor such relationships outside the marriage, since they bring greater enjoyment to life and produce attitudes that usually enrich one's marriage. Still, we all need to stay in tune with what is happening in these casual or ongoing relationships, and this chapter will explore some ways you can enjoy such experiences while maintaining fidelity.

Establish Ground Rules for Behavior

During the premarital consultations I have with couples, I emphasize taking a good look at some of the real issues men and women face during marriage.

"What are the ground rules for your marriage?" I might ask. I'm usually given a puzzled look.

"What are the boundaries of your relationship? Who can do what, when?" Again, a blank stare.

Is it okay for Dennis to take his secretary to dinner on Friday nights after work? Is it permissible for Mary to have dinner with her old college sweetheart, who just happens to be in town?" The look of what in heaven's name is he talking about disappears. Now they understand, but there's also an admission, by most couples, that they have not discussed issues such as these in detail. This is understandable, of course, since most couples about to be married are not apt to speculate about behavior with other men and women. It is uncomfortable to raise an issue that might imply a lack of trust, and few couples venture to take this risk prior to their wedding. They rarely set aside time during courtship to talk honestly about the inevitability of being attracted to someone else. But this attraction is likely to happen during marriage.

It is my hope that people see that it is never too early—and certainly never too late—for those in a committed relationship to establish clear standards of behavior that are mutually understood and approved. I have found that it is not enough for couples to simply affirm a belief in fidelity on their wedding day and then presume that "in-loveness" will carry them through to eternity. Nor can spouses assume that they know each other well enough to be able to predict their extramarital conduct.

One reason marriages fail to work out as smoothly as we might hope is that important ground rules for behavior outside the partnership are established—if at all—on a hit-and-miss basis as the marriage evolves. Generally, guidelines become defined after a crisis develops that forces the issue out in the open. "I never realized that my husband felt it was okay for him to dance close with Betty—I mean really close," lamented a recently divorced mother. "It was not something that I liked, but what can I do now? When I finally talked to him about it, I learned he was in love with her." The inability to or the desire not to clearly state what you feel is appropriate behavior can lead to continual misunderstandings and comments like "I never thought you would do something like that."

Without a set of standards that have been calmly and clearly articulated and negotiated and renegotiated so they meet with acceptance, commitment to the concept of "one

bed, one person, one marriage" may be tentative at best. The
Reverend Morris Samuels, a licensed marriage counselor,
offered an honest personal testimony for the value of setting
ground rules. "I have grown in this process of dealing with
affairs," he told me one day. "There was a time when I encouraged those who were looking for affairs to go ahead and
have them because they felt they needed them for their mental
health or whatever. I said, 'Okay, that is where you are,' and
I supported them in that kind of behavior. But in recent
years I have recognized the disaster that approach has
wrought. I got caught up in the sexual revolution and the
freedom that was implied, but I've found out that people
are a lot more fragile than I thought they were when it comes
to dealing with open marriage and 'do your own thing,' and
for them to enter into that kind of behavior is foolhardy.
Boundary systems must be established, and if people don't
want that kind of restriction in their marriage, I take a hard
line: 'You'd better be damn careful in what you are doing
because very few people can handle the overload an affair
brings.' " Contrary to popular opinion, boundary systems
are not repressive or restrictive but liberating because you
know the framework within which you can operate com-
fortably. If you and your spouse are concerned about laying
down guidelines, and I hope you are, consider these three
important steps:

1. *Do not be afraid to discuss and set limits for involvement with a member of the opposite sex.* Questions like these
may be appropriate:

- Is it okay if I have lunch with my boss? Will that bother
  you?
- Will you be comfortable with my dancing with Cindy
  at the party tomorrow night?
- Is it acceptable for me to have a few drinks and flirt with
  the men in the office on Friday afternoons?

- John and Susan are having a tough time—do you mind if I go to dinner with John just to talk and listen?
- The Carlsons have invited us to their annual Mardi Gras Blastaway. You'll be out of town, but do you mind if I go?
- Jim has asked me to be his partner in the Westside Charity Tennis Tournament—is that okay with you? How about if I go with him to the party afterwards?
- The Christmas office party is next Tuesday. How do you feel about my being there?
- My boss has asked me to travel with her to the annual meeting in Vail, Colorado, and teach her to ski. How do you feel about my doing that?

Some of these hypothetical situations may be perfectly agreeable and easily understood; others may be open to negotiation, while some might send chills of apprehension up and down your spine. For example, the Carlsons have decided they can handle either partner's going on a business trip, just as long as that person comes home on the weekends and restricts weekday activity to business. The husband has also agreed not to worry if his wife goes to lunch with men, but they are committed to keeping the dinner hour for the two of them. She has accepted her husband's drinking and carefree flirting behavior at parties because he has agreed not to go out like this when she is out of town.

The important point to remember is that the option is open for you and your spouse to establish a mutual understanding of extramarital behavior. What is right for you may not be right for your best friend's marriage, but not finding out what is right for you is to be remiss in your marriage.

One couple in my community did not clearly establish ground rules of behavior, and this was partly responsible for the destruction of their marriage. They found that after they had agreed to allow each other independent male-female friendships that neither of them could handle the resulting emotional attachments.

Edith, a forty-six-year-old housewife, became intrigued with the young teacher who taught her son Latin in high school. He understood the difficulties her son was having at school, so she initiated conversations to gain a better perspective on her son's problems. She asked her husband if it was all right if the teacher came over to the house after school. He said sure because he felt nothing could happen in his own house; besides he trusted Edith completely. Even when he noticed that Edith was happier and more talkative on these days when the Latin instructor came to the house, he accepted this level of "dating."

At the same time, Charles, Edith's husband, began going to lunch with a young employee in his insurance firm, which quickly led to his falling in love with her. Edith knew of the lunches but not about his emotional involvement, and she agreed to their continuance. Neither spouse recognized that their extramarital behavior was a threat to the marriage; they naively assumed that they could handle the friendships and that neither would have to worry that their behavior might destroy the marriage. Yet they never made it clear to each other that falling in love and going to bed with their respective friends was not acceptable. Ultimately, they both had a sexual affair—Charles over several months, Edith over a weekend when Charles was out of town. Edith felt her affair was acceptable because it was what she described as a "sexually liberating fling" that would not destroy the marriage. But Charles had his affair, liked it, and wanted to end the marriage. Edith was crushed because they had had different criteria for extramarital behavior and had never checked it out with each other.

2. *Once your standards have been established, step back and try to assess whether they are realistic and workable.* Hypothesis: You and your spouse now expect certain kinds

of behavior that you have negotiated. Are you really able to accept and live up to these standards? Is it realistic to assume, for example, that you can go to the office party, have a few drinks, and walk away from seductive flirting by a fellow worker? If this is not easily handled, perhaps a more logical standard would be to avoid combining alcohol with festive parties.

3. *Once the ground rules have been stated, they need to be discussed, reinforced, and (when necessary) renegotiated at regular intervals.* Individuals change—in their interests, their needs, their outlook—and this brings subtle, sometimes dramatic changes to every marriage. The wise couple will try to accommodate these natural changes by modifying their standards of behavior outside the marriage, for what was appropriate extramarital behavior when the couple was in their thirties may be inappropriate in their forties. The marital "checkups" (which I'll discuss in chapter 11) is an excellent time for reevaluation of this nature.

Naiveté Is Common

In addition to recommending the establishment of ground rules for extramarital behavior, I encourage couples to be aware of their tendencies to be naive about the realities of affairs. One of the best insights I have ever received came from a man I counseled. He is a Los Angeles businessman, an avid outdoorsman, a husband, a father—typical of many of the men in their late thirties whom I know. Faithful for fourteen years and committed to his family and wife, he told me, "You blithely go along in marriage, seemingly happy, and all of a sudden you turn the corner and whammo! you meet another woman, and your life is never the same again—if you let yourself succumb. There's no such thing as a safe person with whom to begin an intimate relationship. When you take that first step, you just can't predict what is going to happen to you. It is a growing thing, and the first step leads to the second and the third."

Even aware, sensitive, intelligent people are taken in by the allure of an affair. Some unfairly test themselves because they feel they control their emotions. But, as my friend was to find out, he could not handle the situation well, and he was naive to assume he could. Ned related how he became attracted to the secretary in his office and how conscious he became of her behavior around him, her attitude, and her appearance. In the beginning their relationship remained at arm's length, but they grew closer and closer. When they began to have sex it was still, he said, "the perfect business deal—sex for sex's sake, nothing more and nothing less. It seems we had a mutual need to continue the relationship; I needed the sex, and I turned her on sexually and emotionally like nobody had done before. I saw her once a week after hours, and there were no strings, no demands, no obligations. The best part was she never asked me to leave my wife."

Ned continued, speaking for countless married people as he described the process: "Our expectation was that it would last a month, maybe two, but it just grew. It was a classic case. I kept thinking it would blow over (I'll just go along for the ride until she gets bored, then I'll go back to where I was), but I began to get even more attracted to her, not just for the sex, but for the whole relationship. We had a phone call that was a turning point; she had a personal problem and I showed empathy. Now our relationship just gets deeper and deeper and we have fallen in love. It shows no sign of going away."

At the time of our last conversation, one and a half years after his affair had begun, Ned's wife had still not learned about it. He feared that discovery was imminent. "People are beginning to suspect something is going on," he said. "You just can't carry on for that long. It's hard to cover your tracks from your friends." Ned is a thoughtful, highly principled person who, like many others, got caught in the web of naiveté and became so entangled in the life of his lover that no clear method of extricating himself was apparent.

Like Ned, most of us do not want to believe we are naive or that we are susceptible to the temptations that overwhelm and conquer others. However, more than one affair that you know about began as the direct result of someone's being unaware of the process taking place. Jane, a newspaper executive who is presently living with a man much older than herself, could look back on two broken marriages with very definite opinions.

"Affairs aren't worth it," she emphasized. "My first marriage, we both were twenty and virgins on our wedding night; at the wedding reception we were pulling ushers and bridesmaids aside, asking them what to do. But we had a strong marriage, or so I thought, with a lot of mutual respect and interests—we looked out the same window at life. I just worshipped my husband, but I needed to be filled up with something, so I found a job in the business department of the local newspaper. One day a man walked through the door to begin work, and soon after that we were assigned together to a special project. We started having lunch together, and the better we got to know each other the more we realized we were compatible intellectually and emotionally. Even though I was married, when he kissed me good night after a late night at the office, everything changed. I didn't know any better, and I let myself fall in love with him. I didn't feel this kind of love for my husband, but I believed in fidelity, and I saw what was going to happen next, so I simply left my husband. I never even leveled with him about why—I just moved in with my boyfriend. We later got married, but we were divorced within a year. Looking back now, I would have never left my first husband had I been more mature. I would not have exposed myself to temptation like I did. I recognize now that I had a special marriage, and I regret that I did what I did."

Use the "Creative No"

By now it should be clear that the power of an affair can be greater than any personal resolve you might have to remain faithful. Setting yourself up to be tempted may be something you are unable to handle. Facing the situation head on may require an expert use of what I call the "creative no." When this little word is used wisely, it can have a powerful and beneficial effect.

While on a trip to New York several years ago I had a rewarding discussion with a forty-year-old woman who was about to be married for the first time. We talked about the choice of words in her wedding service and the importance of words in general. She told me that the most important word in her vocabulary was "no."

"I've been approached many times by men who are or were married," she said, "and the no I learned to use was not just the no to sexual intercourse, but the no to gamesmanship, to dinners with men who belonged elsewhere, to being pushed into relations that I didn't really want. My no, when I used it, told my friends in no uncertain terms that I would not compromise my values or beliefs for momentary pleasure. What was great was that once I learned it was okay to say no, saying yes was much more fun." By saying no creatively, she insured that people did not get hurt. Her no also told others that she was a person who believed in what was right for her and was not afraid to affirm it.

At times I have felt that this book could have been written in just one sentence: "Extramarital sex will not occur if someone says no." Or, as Cervantes once wrote: "No padlocks, bolts, or bars can secure a maiden as her own reserve." However, ours is a yes culture, and learning how and when to say no *creatively* is an art. From our earliest years we are asked to say yes to our parents and other adults when they want us to do something. As we begin the process of dating we are asked—or expected—to go to the movies, hold hands, go parking, touch, kiss, pet, and eventually make love. During college or as we begin work we are expected to say yes to the advances of someone of the opposite sex, especially if he or she has spent money on us with a nice evening of dinner and dancing. Learning to say no is difficult, and the lessons we learn come hard, but eventually the simple realization that it is appropriate to say no to the advances of another person will help preserve fidelity in one's marriage.

Men as well as women must strive for the effective use of the word no. Dick Kreitler, a former successful New York stockbroker, my cousin and good friend, talked freely about the temptations he faced in his office and how he coped: "When you are successful in your midthirties and up, you have a special appeal to younger women because their peers are often floundering and without direction. The older man with power, money, and direction is damn appealing. So this guy finds himself in double jeopardy. Not only is he a target; he himself is attracted to the young women in his office because they are generally freer sexually than his wife (or that's his impression) and they dress in a provocative style. So the bait is always there to take—but it is also easy to fend off. You can find your own way if you want to. My approach is to say, 'Hey, I think you are really attractive, and I'm flattered that you find me appealing, but I'm not interested.' Nip it quick before it has a chance to nip you."

Another perspective is offered by Anne, a legal secretary who came to me with this typical dilemma. "To be honest," she said, "I'm not all that excited about my marriage. My husband is away a lot, and I feel cut off from his life. I think my boss senses this because he's starting to make advances. The other night we worked a little late and he said, 'Let's go have a drink.' We had a good time and he didn't try to go any further, but now I have a feeling right in the pit of my stomach and it won't go away. I realize that I don't *want* to say no if he asks me out again; I'm lonely and I see something appealing." I felt that she wanted me to give her a justification for going out with her boss, but I warned her: "If you value your marriage, you'll know that *now* is the time for the 'creative no'—not after another night of drinks with your boss."

The Ansel Adams Guide

Ansel Adams, the marvelous naturalist photographer, stresses the importance of visualizing a photograph before it is taken. In essence, he encourages the photographer to do some mental homework on lighting contrast, depth of field, and composition before squeezing the shutter. This same approach may be borrowed for our purposes. By previsualizing situations in which you are going to encounter members of the opposite sex, you will be better able to handle the emotions and the feelings that may surface in those meetings—and also the possible advances of others.

Let's say, for example, that Carl and Alice are throwing a Fourth of July toga party to celebrate the completion of their new swimming pool. You and your spouse both know that wine, water, song, togas, and a warm evening mix very well. So take a moment to previsualize what that could mean to you. What might the picture include? Who will be there? Will *she* (or *he*) be there—the man or woman you find particularly appealing? What will you drink and how much? What will happen if she *is* there and the two of you drink too much and your wife is busy and this other woman wants to dance with you? Asking questions beforehand might prevent having to answer tougher questions later on.

It would be nice if God had created us with an internal will power so highly developed that we could handle any extramarital encounter and fend off temptation with ease. But as Andrew Greeley states in *Sexual Intimacy*, "Rejecting the offer of a new body requires courage and strength." So

if you don't have the power to use the creative no immediately, learn to draw a clear mental picture of those times
when you might encounter someone new and stimulating
who could become an eventual bed partner. This will help
diffuse the energy of the moment when that person does come
along.

The Reverend Pittman McGehee, the respected Dean
of the Cathedral in Houston, is a perceptive man who is fully
aware of the standards he has set for himself as a counselor.
He told me how he uses previsualization in his role as people-
helper. "I'm aware of my sexual makeup and what triggers
strong sexual feelings. When I'm confronted with this situation in my office, I make a conscious compensation, because I
really want to be of help to the women who come to see me.
If an attractive woman is coming to me for personal guidance,
she's in a vulnerable position and I'll remind myself 'This is
really going to be tough for me. I need to think about what
it will be like with her in my office.' I look and listen to my
own internal system and that helps."

We have all felt that urge propelling us toward another
person, and previsualizing can help many of us deal constructively with our feelings, like Dean McGehee, and in a
humorous way, like the psychiatrist depicted in a cartoon in
Medical Aspects of Human Sexuality. The respectable looking doctor was seated near a curvacious, mini-skirted woman
on his couch, and he could be seen strapping himself into
the chair with a seat belt. That's previsualization.

Touch Magic

If you fail to anticipate or previsualize a particular situation, and your naiveté has led you into an exciting but uncomfortable encounter, and the word no won't come to your
lips, then be extremely sensitive to the power of touch. Affairs
in their beginning stages encourage touch, and brief touch
may cause a powerful, transforming sensation within you.

"My affair started over lunch," recalls Jenny, a recep-
tionist who had been married for three years. "Four of us
from the office happened to get together one day—two men
and two women—and I enjoyed the chance to get to know
Jason better. I knew I was attracted to him, but I never
dreamed it would lead anywhere. Anyway, I remember that I
ordered a large salad, and when Jason asked if I wanted
something to drink, he reached across the table and touched
my hand. I felt this profound tingling sensation, something
I hadn't felt with my husband since before we were married.
Still, I never envisioned myself going to bed with Jason. I was
married. But the more we touched around the office, on
coffee breaks, at lunch, the more I liked it, and the more I
wanted to get closer to his body—in bed."

Touch is important to us, and if it is not a part of your
daily married life, be prepared to deal with its power over you
from people outside the marriage. Especially in social settings
where there is good company, good food, good wine, and good
music, "close encounters" are likely to occur, either while
dancing, conversing on the couch, or standing and talking. In
fact, dancing is probably the most socially acceptable form
of sexual relating in our culture, and it can loosen a lot of
inhibitions. Do not underestimate how mysteriously magical
and intimate the power of touch can be.

To Flirt or Not to Flirt

As we learn to live with the fact that we are sexual
creatures and that much of our behavior is sexual, flirting
can be a playful, artful part of interpersonal relationships—
and it can get us into deep trouble. I love to flirt, and I like
it when a woman flirts with me, but I'm also sensitive to the
"fickle factor of flirting" and to what it may foreshadow. I've
known too many affairs that can trace their beginnings to
simple flirtation that goes unchecked.

We all flirt in our own way, but what counts is knowing

how to do so without conquering or being seduced. *Healthy flirting means giving attention to another person without intending to carry that relationship into the bedroom.* Such flirting behavior among social and working acquaintances may involve warm, kidding, or joking behavior, with possible sexual overtones. This type of natural interchange is common today, and if honest and open, these moments of delightful intimacy are shared and cherished: the lingering, knowing smiles of appreciation, the spontaneous embraces, the pats, the caresses—all contribute to making certain relationships special.

Unfortunately, flirting, as it relates to marriage, has a bad reputation. During our dating and courtship years, open interaction with the opposite sex is generally encouraged by parents, and we are allowed to flirt because it is seen as a natural and healthy part of growing up. But, once we are engaged, old familiar behavior patterns are suddenly discouraged or forbidden. That common feeling of marital possessiveness and an unwillingness to trust casts a negative light on flirting. Even flirting with one's spouse often disappears, to the detriment of the marriage.

Instead of fearing flirting, we need to regard it as a natural part of our human expression and to channel it into healthy directions. A good first step is for you to continually evaluate your own flirting behavior, since you have control over your own actions. For example, we know it's fun to have eye contact with another person at a party, but are your eyes saying a friendly "Hello—I'd like to get to know you better" or are they saying "Do you want to go to bed?" Are you aware of how you use your body to communicate with others in a social situation? Are you flirting for personal gain, hoping that someone will take your subtle suggestions and run with them? I have found that most women are not dummies when it comes to flirting men. They understand the difference between flirting and hustling, and they know when a man is "on the make," when the hand of friendship is really the arm of seduction. Of course, some men and women like this type of game playing, but I regard it as the unhealthy side of flirting behavior when it involves a married person.

In studying the art of flirting, I have learned that it can sometimes be misunderstood. A doctor friend told me how he got into a delicate situation by innocently flirting with a woman on his hospital staff. "I didn't intend for anything to happen," he said, "but she did. I didn't realize we were coming from two different places." He just wanted to add a little zest to his working day, but she wanted to have an affair, and she tried for weeks afterwards to seduce him until he finally had to tell her bluntly that he had no interest in going beyond their present relationship.

Flirting behavior may be misinterpreted or threatening to some people, so be careful. I went to a party one evening and was introduced to a woman who wrote children's books— and who also happened to be a statuesque, raven-haired beauty. We began to talk in earnest about her writing, and I couldn't help being stimulated by her energy, her beauty, and her intelligence. We had been enjoying each other's company and flirting in a delightful manner when I began to notice her husband glancing our way with obvious discomfort as he tried to remain interested in the conversation he was having. I recognized that he was viewing my behavior with his wife as intention rather than attention, and had that been the case, his jealousy would have been justified; he did not know who I was and whether I intended anything beyond the dialogue. So at the first opportunity I asked Sandy to introduce me to her husband, and I made a special effort to ease his mind. I expressed my feelings about his wife's writing and complimented him on his good taste. I then introduced him to my wife to show that I was committed to somebody else.

Perhaps flirting is something we learn from others. If this is so, I learned from my grandfather Kreitler, who was an expert on this behavior. He always expressed a genuine interest in women, he could laugh and kid with them, and he listened in such a way that they all felt he appreciated what they had to offer. He was the epitome of the man who delighted in all women—from the secretaries in his office to the ladies in his neighborhood—but he let everyone know that he knew the difference between all other women and his wife, who was always number one. That is the art of flirting.

Extramarital Friendships

Encouraging extramarital friendships is for me a pleasant task that is spoiled only by the realization that friends sometimes ruin everything—their friendship *and* the marriage (or marriages) involved—by falling in love with one another. I'll suggest some important steps that can help prevent this, but I'll first explain why I feel such extramarital relationships are necessary in most marriages.

Ideally, the important needs for sex, affection, love, freedom to grow, and affirmation of one's worth are met in the marriage. Yet considering it realistically, wives and husbands are usually unable to meet all the supplemental needs of their spouses, and I believe it is naive and unrealistic to expect that they can. *Even in the best of marriages, there is a genuine need for other male-female relations.* Said psychologist Isabelle Fox of the Western Psychological Center in Los Angeles in *Women's Day*: "If a partner has certain nonsexual needs that you cannot meet, one way to guard against a potential affair is to allow him or her to fill them outside of marriage. When we are free to form legitimate relations with others—a mutual interest in opera, football, poetry, jogging . . . we are not likely to use them to harm the marriage."

When couples are able to trust each other as they develop good extramarital friendships, not only their own personal development but the health of the marriage is enhanced.

Caroline, who has been married to a writer in Los Angeles for twenty years, openly enjoys her friendships with males. "In addition to my husband, I have several men friends who affirm me," she said. "They tell me I'm attractive, not just in a physical sense but as a person—and that's good for my self-esteem. But the best part is that I can bring back what I have gained to my marriage. Sharing the ideas and interests of others with my husband has been of value to us both." Rather than judging or condemning her husband for not being able to meet certain of her needs, Caroline accepted her autonomy and realized she alone was responsible for her happiness. She confided in me that when she and her husband realized that they were not solely responsible for making each other happy, it freed them to pursue and delight in their own interests. Caroline has not had an affair with any of her men friends, and yet like many of us who have strong friendships with members of the opposite sex, she has had to make it clear on occasion what she considers is part of a friendship and what is not. Her use of the creative no has been an important ally, and the yes to friendship has been openly and honestly expressed.

REMAINING FRIENDS WHILE NOT BECOMING LOVERS

Dr. Warren Moulton, a counselor and therapist from Kansas City, asks the $64,000 question: "Can you let those people who are close friends be a vital part of your life without threatening the intimacy you have and cherish with your spouse?" The answer is yes you can, but the chances are probably better than fifty-fifty that you (or your partner) will fall in love with someone else during your marriage. I recognize the inevitability of strong personal attachments for a particular person, but I emphasize that you do not have to act on these feelings in a sexual manner. By and large, we are not responsible for our "love" feelings—they happen and they are neither right nor wrong. But we are responsible for our actions. *It is what you do with the feelings you have for a friend or work partner that is the concern of this book.*

Following are a few practical hints that may help you maintain your cherished friendships while ensuring the sanctity of your marriage commitment.

• Most of your good friends will pose little or no threat to your marriage because a brother-sister type of relationship develops. Yet there are certain people who should raise your red flag of caution because they are sexually attractive to you. We all find a particular type of person more appealing than others. This person may be tall, blond, and extroverted, or short, bearded, and highly introverted—or any combination of characteristics. Some of us drool over the Paul Newman type or the Candice Bergen look; others of us may find Suzanne Somers or Kenny Rogers our type. Whatever, there is usually someone in our circle of friends who has that special sexual appeal that "turns us on." He or she may have goddess-like or godlike qualities that we respond to almost automatically. If you are with a person like this who triggers those palpitations or stomach flutters, then flirting and enjoying special moments of conversational intimacy must be carefully handled. States Carlfred B. Broderick, co-director of the Marriage and Family Counseling Center at the University of Southern California: "If you find yourself in a situation involving delicious privacy with an attractive member of the opposite sex, you should begin to look for ways to restructure the situation."

Perhaps you might also follow the advice of the Reverend Morris Samuels, who counsels: "One of the things that I really stress with people is the ability to be intimate with friends without having to go to bed. An important step is to recognize another person's sexual attraction and to acknowledge that attraction. Be up front about it. Raise up to a level of discussion those qualities you find appealing, and sublimate or back off from the physical expression of those feelings. I like a woman I play tennis with because she gives me a darn good game and she is fun to talk with. She's a good friend, and I may buy her a drink once in a while, but I don't want to get past that. I don't want to jeopardize the friendship we have."

• Backyard counseling, over-the-fence counseling, around-the-water-cooler counseling, and over-a-drink-at-a-bar counseling are popular American pastimes, but watch out because such a process can produce unexpected results.

Being a good listener and a supportive friend is a wonderful quality. Time and time again, people in my office have cited that special friend who has taken time to listen and offer a shoulder to lean on. Good friends with whom we can communicate easily and openly are hard to find, and if you are such a person, be sensitive to the fact that you are an appealing friend. Your counseling or advice may have real merit and it may be the needed balm to soothe a troubled heart. In either case, the sharing of personal, intimate feelings and facts tends to make the speaker and the hearer extremely close. Unfortunately, in some cases, this closeness results in the following scenario: "We were simply listening to each other's problems at home—the problems he was having with his wife, and the problems I was having with my husband. There was a much-needed listening post at the other end of the phone. We discovered we had so much in common that it was natural to start making excuses to spend time together. The next thing I knew we were in love, and there was no going back."

Another insight is provided by Carlfred Broderick in an article about preserving fidelity in *Medical Aspects of Human Sexuality*: "I am convinced that more people get themselves into the pain of infidelity through empathy, concern, and compassion than through any base motive. The world is full of lonely and vulnerable people, hungry for a sympathetic ear and shoulder to cry on." He continues by illustrating the process that takes place: "With a little help from rationalization, the sympathy leads smoothly to tenderness, the

tenderness to the need for privacy, the privacy to physical
consolation, and the consolation straight to bed."

These two statements illustrate the importance not only
of being selective about your confidants but of being up front
with those people who see you as a confidant. When you
require a sympathetic ear, try to be aware of the other person's needs. And during your own periods of stress and
change, remember that your ability to offer objective counsel
to a friend of the opposite sex may be compromised. In fact,
my experience has shown that during times of particular
vulnerability in either your life or the life of a friend, it is
best to seek friends of the same sex or professional counselors
of either sex. Even though you feel you can provide objective,
caring counsel to a friend of the opposite sex, it may be wise
to say no to eliminate some of the difficult situations that are
bound to occur as you develop a closer friendship. Diffusing
a potential time bomb with the person you find sexually attractive may be one of the best gifts you can ever give your
marriage.

• Another point to consider as you struggle to keep those
special friendships from changing into a love affair is the
advice given me by the mother of three boys who came close
to an affair with a man who had been her closest confidant:
"When lovers run out of things to say, they speak with their
bodies. In close extramarital friendships, it's tempting when
the conversation dies to start touching, because that also is a
very direct form of communication. Friendships change into
physical relations when the two people lose the art of dialogue." Friends should gain their enjoyment and gratification
from stimulating conversations or the sharing of mutual interests—whether it's classical music, jogging, tennis, or landscape design. When men and women fail to put a premium on
the superb pleasure and growth that can be derived from
interesting dialogue and shared experiences, the human
tendency is often to act out the warm, close feelings via their
hands, arms, and bodies.

• Beware of the next step when your original purpose for getting to know a certain person begins to change. We tend to choose friends of the opposite sex for their sense of humor, common interests, and similar values. I call this process "friendship specializing," because usually only one or two such friends among all our acquaintances are set aside for special attention and treatment. Their unique appeal to us may be their "sexy mind," their ability to discuss and argue about a variety of subjects, their interest in contemporary photography, the opera, racquetball, or Chinese calligraphy. The key is to stick to these original reasons for pursuing and nurturing close friendships, and you will decrease the potential for an affair.

I am unquestionably affirming the maintenance of good male-female friendships. In our culture today, lovers are easier to find than good friends. Friends who become lovers sacrifice something that is hard to find, difficult to maintain, and often impossible to replace.

CHAPTER 9

Marriage and Life's Crossroads

We will all be confronted by significant crossroads as we live our marriage: advancing age, bodily changes, pregnancy, a work-related move, the wife joining or rejoining the work force, children leaving the nest. If we choose to underplay the importance of these times of upheaval and transition—to the point of even avoiding an awareness of how they can affect our marriage—we may unwittingly leave the door open to the powerful allure of an affair.

My purpose in this chapter is not to repeat well-documented information on why certain times in an adult's life are likely to bring changes in behavior and outlook but to show how these times can lead to the germination of affairs. Many men and women make the right decisions as they work through and adjust to the crossroads in their marriage. Yet many other married people are unable to make their journey through these difficult passages without turning to an extramarital lover to ease their pain, frustration, or disenchantment.

In a series of lectures on human sexuality, Dr. Urban T. Holmes observed that "if one comes to wholeness he must pass by evil. We wrestle with demons before we embrace angels." Even as we strive for affair prevention, most all of us will still have close brushes with the temptation of extramarital sex. Your spouse is also traveling this path in his or her life. When both of you have that awareness and you can openly discuss what this means in terms of your marriage and the other men and women in your life, you will be able to confront your crossroads in a healthy, realistic manner.

The Mileposts of Aging

I have found that aging threatens even the most secure person and that few people accept the arrival of their birthday with equanimity. Each succeeding birthday has its own assets and liabilities, but in terms of extramarital affairs the milestone birthdays of thirty, forty, and fifty seem to produce the most anxiety and soul searching. Turning the corner to embrace another ten years is sobering.

AGE 50

Fifty has been described as the beginning of the downhill side of life, and the decade that it portends is often faced with apprehension. This seems especially true among men, many of whom start a personal-appraisal process: Am I a good person? Am I at a plateau? Have I contributed? Am I loved? Am I enjoying life? Some men are pleased with what they discover, and they renew their commitment to their family, job, religion, and friends because they value consistency and stability. But others find the answers and the insights depressing. They see their life slipping away from them, and they take a good hard look at their marriage and think "I want more out of life than I'm getting. I'm not satisfied, and I will find someone to bring me greater happiness."

In addition, there's great appeal to that one last fling to ward off the punishment of aging. One attractive fifty-one-year-old actor who had worked hard to keep himself in shape complained of creeping old age and how hard it was to stay young. He resented his wife's health problems, which prevented them from sharing much sex, and he admitted he was courting younger women to ease his frustration. "My wife wasn't giving me the strokes I needed as I saw fifty come and go," he said. "I kept telling her I needed more than I was getting, but she couldn't and wouldn't go along with me. So I've turned to the young ladies, and it's good for my ego."

It is understandable for men and women like this to have strong feelings for persons of the opposite sex, but I hope most of us can have the type of marriage in which, by the age of fifty, we can look at another person's body and appreciate the attractiveness but avoid the temptation to go beyond the looking stage.

AGE 40

The beginning of this time-is-running-out decade has become a significant rite of passage in our culture, especially for married men. When I was writing this chapter, three men I know well were having affairs. Their stated reasons differed, but a common denominator was their age: forty or forty-one. The mystique that surrounds this particular age is clearly manifested by the way men and women respond to a man's fortieth birthday. For example, my good friend Robert Hillman ordered personalized license plates, RDH 40, when he crossed that magic line. Another friend's wife threw a party titled "The Last Hurrah," while the friends of Dan Martin really went all out. Twelve of them traveled with him to Sun Valley for a week of skiing and a celebration of his birthday. An enormous amount of planning went into the trip, and when the group arrived in downtown Sun Valley, signs and posters proclaiming DAN MARTIN IS 40 graced every corner.

Wives are perhaps even warier than husbands about hitting forty. Commented writer Norman Lobsenz in *Women's Day*: "In recent years several men I know reached their fortieth birthday, and their wives gave them a surprise birthday party. When my friend Alan was approaching that milestone I asked his wife if she was going to do the same. 'Certainly not,' Elaine said. 'Every man I know who had a fortieth birthday party went out and started an affair the next month.'"

Obviously men have affairs in their early thirties, but most are often absorbed by the upward spiral of their career during this decade, and it's not until the late thirties that they begin to stop and take a deeper look at their lives. They also begin to view the temptations and opportunities that have always been around them at work in a different light. At thirty, a man might see the office girl as a friend and an attractive person, but he generally doesn't size her up in terms of having an affair because he's happily married and is more concerned about how she can help him get the job done so he can advance up the ladder. By age forty, however, he has changed and his marriage has changed. The same attractive women are around the office, but he may now begin to view them in specific sexual terms.

AGE 30

Here my focus shifts from men to women, for it has been my experience that the years from thirty to thirty-five can be every bit as treacherous for married women as it is for men turning forty. When a woman hits thirty (or slightly beyond that, given later marriage and childbirth), the realization hits that she is a woman and no longer a recent college student or a young bride. The newness of marriage has faded, and if her children are off to school she is beginning to awaken to her own needs. "I'm really ripe for an affair," admitted a thirty-one-year-old housewife who had come to talk to me about her faltering marriage. "I feel trapped, caged, stifled—everything's for my kids, my husband, or my relatives, and there's nothing for me. I know I sound selfish, but I've been a good mother and a faithful wife, and right now I want somebody to give me attention and affection."

A woman in Kansas City who was married to a young attorney came to the similar realization that she needed more than PTA meetings, car pools, and neighborhood get-togethers to give meaning to her life. "I never finished school because I had to work to put Carl through law school," she said. "I missed a lot, and now I'm going after it." She began taking night classes with a vengeance, which led to secret meetings with an older man—and eventually to the disintegration of her marriage.

The crossroad of age will be a different experience for each of us. Some of us may awaken at twenty-eight, thirty-seven, forty-three, fifty-five, or sixty-eight and ask "What are my life and my marriage all about?" Be aware that the time will come for you, if it has not already arrived, and that you'll probably do some serious thinking about your marriage and your life.

Dealing with Body Changes

We have to contend not only with a psychological awareness that the years are rolling by but with the hormonal and physical changes that occur. We are asked to love each other without qualifications, but this ideal is difficult to live up to when one's spouse puts on weight, loses hair, acquires a chronic illness, or loses that youthful vitality that once encouraged closeness and sexual relations. Working through these physical obstacles requires stamina, love, and courage, but by failing to accept the reality of aging gracefully you may undermine your marriage and increase the temptation to stray.

An example is offered by Paul, a thirty-nine-year-old, happily married insurance salesman who came to me confused and frustrated by the feelings he had for his wife. After the birth of their third child she had to have a complete hysterectomy, which led to a natural decrease in her sexual drive. She was also apprehensive about every sexual experience because she had lost the ability to lubricate easily and found sex painful. "My wife only goes through the motions," said Paul. "I know she does not feel anything toward me sexually, and I'm tempted to pursue a young lady at my office who I know likes me. What should I do?" I talked to Paul about the fact that he faced a significant crossroad in life, where one of three decisions had to be made, each with its own cost, and its own promise.

1. He could accept the situation as it was. COST: no sex at the level he desired. PROMISE: living with a good wife, mother, and companion.

2. He could choose to have an affair. COST: might jeopardize his marriage. PROMISE: better and more frequent sex.

3. He and his wife could get medical and emotional support. COST: there might be the immediate pain of hearing things that are hard to hear. PROMISE: both partners would be working toward a mutually satisfying and acceptable sexual relationship.

Paul chose to seek help for himself, as a way to gain a better understanding and acceptance of his wife's changes. She fortunately called her doctor, who was sensitive to her needs, offered a prescription, and recommended sexual counseling.

Pregnancy and Postpartum

Ideally, husbands and wives draw closer together during the months of anticipation before the birth of their child. The sense of joy and excitement should offset any of the attending difficulties. But counselors and therapists are well aware that even for the well-adjusted couple, the period of pregnancy and the months after a baby is born can often bring stress to the marriage—sometimes to the breaking point. This tension may open the door to "quick fix" sex in the form of a fling, or it might pave the way for a long-term affair.

A typical situation is illustrated by the exasperated housewife who told me, "How could my husband do this to me? Here I am, eight months pregnant with his child, and I discover he's off with some chick in San Francisco. I know I've shut him off from sex—it's damn uncomfortable when you feel like you're carrying a watermelon in your belly—but I thought he could handle a couple of months without intercourse. Boy, was I wrong."

Not only does pregnancy produce sexual discomfort or irritation for many women, but a pregnant wife may lose her appeal in the eyes of her husband. As a result, satisfying sex may not be easily shared over a long period of time before and after birth. Here's where special patience and caring are demanded and where means of expressing love other than intercourse may be required. Kissing, caressing, holding, and nurturing are vital expressions of support and love in any relationship, but to demonstrate this closeness during pregnancy may mean the difference between a partner's remaining faithful and his straying. Perceptive advice was offered by a man who has assisted with the birth of all three of his children. "Get help for your marriage when it is needed," he said. "Make changes at the point when there are little irritations but you are still thinking of nobody but your wife. Wipe the slate clean each morning, especially during the later stages of her pregnancy."

The actual birth of a child may force further adaptations of prepregnancy behavior patterns and more effective methods of coping. Wrote Dr. David Youngs, in an article titled "Postpartum Sexual Problems": "The husband may feel frustrated by the limited sexual opportunities offered at this time and in addition may feel rejected by his wife, who is increasingly preoccupied with the new baby. Sexual infidelity by the husband appears to be significantly increased during this period." Awareness of the impact of a birth on your marriage is the first step in formulating a method to cope with the change.

"I've Been Moved" (I.B.M.)

Timing is often a crucial ingredient contributing to an affair's beginning. Let us presume for a moment that you have found yourself bored by sex with your spouse and that communication in your marriage has deteriorated. Mix these ingredients with a decision by your corporation to move you from Chicago to Cleveland. Such a move could energize your marriage, but the chances are much greater that you and your spouse will face much stress. Marital problems are just as portable as the furniture, and the added burdens associated with your change of residence can often prove overwhelming. Fortunately, corporations that once moved employees with little regard for the attending trauma are now more conscious of the many needs that arise. Steps are often taken by corporations to ease the transition, but a couple must still rely on its own inner strength to work through the problems that uprooting brings.

If the husband is the working spouse, his job usually offers immediate friendships and a built-in support system. The wife, however, is required to focus time and energy on moving into a new house, finding new schools, learning her way around a new community, and making new friends. Putting all this together may be exciting and challenging, but it often brings depression and loneliness because there is no one with whom to share the process.

At this crossroad, the perceptive and caring husband makes that extra effort to tell his wife, over and over, how she is appreciated for all the important work she is doing to make the transition. He might also ensure ways of meeting new people by encouraging ties with community organizations, neighborhood groups, churches and synagogues, and business friends who have children of similar ages. And the wife will recognize that her husband needs an extra boost when he comes home at night. Changing jobs or moving up the corporate ladder is stimulating and exciting but also anxiety producing and psychologically draining. When married partners can recognize their *mutual vulnerability* at critical times like this, they can take care to keep the path clear for positive adjustments that strengthen rather than weaken their marriage.

A smart couple will also learn to have something left over for each other at the end of the day. The reserved energy that we all have but rarely use is an essential need during any I.B.M. transition period. Emotions such as resentment, anger, and bitterness may easily surface during a move, but when an effort is made to balance them with love and a concern for each other's "ness" needs, the appeal of other men and women is greatly minimized.

The Wife's Entering or Re-Entering the Work Force

Much has been written about the demands made on a marriage when the wife goes to work after years of raising the kids and managing the household. My concern here is how a couple handles this crossroad in their marriage in terms of relating to each other as husband and wife—and thus how they cope with affair prevention.

Caroline Bird, in her book *The Two Paycheck Marriage,* cautions that "the act of earning her own paycheck changes a woman's powers in a marriage, her attitude toward her family and herself, her sexual interests, her assertiveness, even her conversation." Money in and of itself is neither good nor evil—but the possession of it does bring power, and it will bring a new dimension to the marriage. Also, the pursuit of that earning power brings women in closer contact with more men. Statistics indicate that because of this greater accessibility to men, women in the work force are more susceptible to having an affair than women who do not work. Says Rona Lee Cohen, co-director of Seminars in Sexuality in Los Angeles, "Women out in the world are now exposed more to men, and not knowing how to handle this from the inside will sometimes choose the path of least resistance—the affair."

A husband who is not completely secure will often feel threatened when he knows his spouse is going to have the same sexual opportunities he has had for years. In part, this fear stems from his having witnessed what goes on among his peers or from his having violated his own marital covenant. Typical of the resulting bias against women in the work world is the statement by a friend who said, "I certainly do not want my wife working. I work hard to afford her everything she needs, so why should she need to work?" Perhaps he feared his wife's job would be the first step in a process that would lead to an affair.

My own belief is that it is unhealthful to approach this marital turning point with fear and trepidation. I've found that in most cases, a woman's sense of self-esteem and the male friendships she makes at work can enrich her life—and subsequently her marriage. Broadening her circle of relations is stimulating and educating, and her new male and female friends can become an important support system in addition to her husband and family. Her experience away from the home often clarifies her commitment to her family, and the new sense of worthiness that results from all this usually makes a transient love affair far less appealing.

In my own marriage, I learned firsthand about the adjustments required by a wife's entering the work force. After an eleven-year hiatus, during which her primary focus was on nurturing our two children, my wife, Edon, went back to work nearly full-time. Her working suddenly meant that the time I used to take for granted, when she was always around home, disappeared, and we had to learn to make our time together high quality. One good habit we developed was making sure we "checked calendars" every day and for the weeks ahead, setting aside time for each other and coordinating our free time as well as our busy time. For example, if I knew in advance that Edon was going to work late on a particular night, I tried to schedule a business obligation for the same evening. We also made a conscious effort to go to bed at the same time. We were so busy during the day that we didn't want to be like two ships passing in the night, as so often happens in hectic households in which one spouse goes to bed early while the other stays up watching television or reading. Another important part of our daily life was to set aside time to share feelings and to make sure that the new feelings brought about by her job were articulated and understood by both of us.

CHAPTER 10

Affair Tip-Offs and Confrontation

Most men over thirty know the early warning signals for heart attacks, and most women know the danger signs of breast cancer. But what about the tip-offs that can flag a potential extramarital affair—your own or your spouse's? What are some of the behavior patterns you can look for that might indicate your vulnerability to an affair or your spouse's actual involvement with another person? And then how should you bring these feelings—or suspicions—to the surface so they can be openly confronted?

We are now familiar with many of the reasons *why* people have affairs, and successful prevention involves an awareness of these reasons and their tell-tale signs. My purpose in this chapter is to highlight many of these early indications so you can step back and look at your own behavior (or that of your spouse) and perhaps realize "Hey, wait a minute— this is happening to my marriage."

To reiterate an earlier warning: don't let naiveté blind you. Men and women often have difficulty accepting and acknowledging the early signals of an affair because they naively believe "No, it couldn't happen to me" or "My partner would never hurt me like that." Yet practically all people who have told me about their affairs can look back and isolate that moment when they realized something special was happening to them. They even admit to me, "Peter, I wish I had known what those feelings really meant and where they would lead me. I just didn't realize." It can be hard to accept the possibility that adultery may become a viable option in your marriage, but a denial of the signals may mean that when acceptance comes, it is too late to stop the process. So open your eyes to see your marital relationship as it really exists; get in touch with your feelings and trust your senses. By doing so, you will perceive more clearly the signals that may already be present in your marriage.

Tip-Offs in Your Own Behavior

In her book *Every Other Man*, Dr. Mary Ann Bartusis declares that "a change in behavior patterns is the single most important early warning signal that something is happening that may affect your marriage." I agree with this concept, and I would add the fact that most people admit they have felt a "vulnerability" to an affair before it happened. Following is advice from people who have reflected on the signals that indicated they were moving toward an affair.

1. *Regardless of the reasons that actually lead people into an affair, a process I call drifting often sets everything into motion.* "I feel myself drifting away from my husband," comments a thirty-two-year-old housewife. "Even when he's around, my mind is preoccupied with more interesting thoughts." Drifting can be described as moving aimlessly through your marriage with an attitude of "que será, será"— what will be, will be—and letting yourself be carried along by circumstance. Every marriage maintains a holding pattern periodically, but if this feeling of going through the motions becomes a recurring pattern, you may drift right into another relationship.

Drifting usually indicates that you have quit actively participating in your marriage and you have decided (perhaps unconsciously) that you are not going to exert any real effort to make the marriage worth something. In such a situation, you may be seeking the affection of someone else, or your emotional energy may already be directed elsewhere, to someone you have found who cares for you and for whom you care more than you care for your spouse. Be sensitive to these inner messages that warn of drifting. It's okay if they happen only occasionally, but if they become persistent, the "drift" has become a threat to the survival of your marriage.

2. *Are you creating excuses to continually visit with someone in your work environment, neighborhood, social club, or organization?* My friend Frank had several affairs during his first marriage, and I asked him to give me the major clue as to when the process of affair development began for him. "The first sign is when you start making excuses to be with another woman," he said without hesitation, "and I don't mean to be in bed, but just to be with her and talk with her. I think the minute you are arranging so that you can be someplace together, and you can't wait to see her, that's it folks. And that's way before you wind up in bed."

Adults who are beginning to have special feelings for a person outside their marriage know all too well the many games that are played to make contact with this person. It may be a subtle change in one's pattern of walking around the office, taking coffee breaks at a particular time, biking around the neighborhood, or altering one's jogging route— anything to facilitate a "chance encounter" and a subsequent conversation. One executive said he found himself making excuses to give work to a particular secretary who was especially attractive to him; a young lawyer admitted she began targeting an older man in her office by joining him in his noontime passion: going to art exhibits; and a bored housewife gave an intimate dinner party to celebrate her husband's recent promotion, but the real reason, she admitted, was so she could sit next to Ken, the young bachelor surgeon who had recently moved into their neighborhood.

3. *How are you handling repetitive contact with a par-*

ticular person in a working, social, or sporting situation? Strong male-female friendships bring great joy and satisfaction, but frequent togetherness can bring increasing intimacy and the potential for an affair. The experience of Janice serves as an appropriate warning. For three years she and her husband, Jack, played social tennis with George and Clair. This also included regular dinners out, family get-togethers with the kids, and church functions. Constant contact and increasing closeness brought greater knowledge of one another and eventually spelled the end of two marriages and the beginning of two others. "I really knew deep down that I was not handling all the contact with Clair and George that well," said Janice. "Frankly, I was spending more quality time with George than my husband, and I kept making excuses for us to get together—not because I enjoyed Clair all that much, but because I loved being around George. I should have known better, but all of a sudden—wham!— I was in love with him, and I couldn't stay away from him."

When it comes to male-female friendships, a married person must have a good self-understanding to successfully handle frequent contact with an extramarital friend. You must be ready to deal with the power of that repeated association.

4. *Are you finding yourself preoccupied by your thoughts for another person?* Absentminded behavior—that "off in the clouds" sensation—often accompanies the initial phase of falling in love. In terms of affairs, mothers have been known to forget their children's lunch for school, burn the toast, forget the cleaning, or thoroughly mess up appointments because of a preoccupation with a particular person who has just entered their lives. One woman told me, "It's damn hard to serve beef Wellington to your spouse when you are falling in love with some other guy. I'd just as soon give my husband hash." Men on the job might act out this preoccupation by looking aimlessly out the window, passing over the pile of "must-do's" repeatedly, or botching up simple routine tasks.

Whatever the situation, such preoccupation may be a sub-
stantial signal to a self-observant person that the climate is
fertile for an affair.

5. *How and why you exchange gifts with a close friend
of the opposite sex—and the type of gift exchanged—may
indicate a developing intimacy.* The giving and receiving of
small gifts is a source of pleasure among friends, but the
selection and timing of those gifts will in part define the
relationship you have. People courting each other or having
an affair enjoy exchanging symbols of their love—a book
of poetry or verse, flowers, a piece of jewelry, slightly risqué
cards, or unique personal items. Selecting the right present,
regardless of its intrinsic value, takes time and thought.
Lovers do not give garden tools or crock pots; they offer
personal items that mean a great deal to the other person. So
it may help to ask yourself what message you're attempting
to communicate via a personal exchange of gifts with your
friend. Here's an experience offered by a woman in my
church. "I couldn't help myself," she exclaimed in utter disbelief as we talked about the development of her affair.
"There I was, in Bullocks, trying to find an appropriate
birthday gift for my husband's business partner—my best
friend's husband—and I spent more damn time selecting
that one silly gift than I'd ever spent getting something for
my husband. I guess in retrospect I should have realized—
I really liked the guy more than I thought."

6. *Has the telephone become an important medium in
your relationship with a friend outside your marriage?* Those
who recall the initial stages of their affair often mention their
repetitive use of the telephone as an important tip-off. This
makes sense. It is not always possible to arrange the so-called
chance encounter, but using the telephone to engage another
in conversation is fast and direct—and you do not have to
leave the privacy of your home. The telephone is personal
enough to allow people to explore a new relationship—to
communicate their feelings, attitudes, and ideas—without

having to deal with eye-to-eye contact or detection by other people. So beware of your use of Ma Bell; it may signal a deepening intimacy that is being nourished by the telephone.

7. *Are you consciously putting yourself into situations where you can increase your chances of meeting someone who might become more than an extramarital friend?* I recall a friend, John, who was forty-two, married, and never missed a Sunday service, though I noticed he always came alone, without his wife or kids. I asked him about this one day and his honesty was admirable. "You may not believe this," he said, "and I'm embarrassed to tell you, but the reason I always come alone and sit at the rear of the church is so I can get a better look at the younger women who might be available." He said he was consciously aware his marriage was in trouble, and he was actively "testing the waters" in the parish, using that conversation time after the Sunday service to find a woman with whom he might pursue a relationship.

One middle-aged man I knew joined a racquetball club, ostensibly to lose weight and lessen his chances of a heart attack. But he soon realized that his real motive was not so much physical fitness as making himself more appealing to the opposite sex. "When I began looking at the younger women and then at my stomach, I knew why I was motivated to change my routine. After about three months a great-looking lady asked me to play racquetball. I had hoped this would happen and it did, but I really wasn't ready for the whole deal. We began to play once a week, and I should have quit right then, but pretty soon we were seeing each other at the club almost every day. I got in great shape, but it ruined my marriage."

8. *What is your body language telling potential lovers?* Consciously or unconsciously, we communicate with our body in working and social situations. And to a person who's receptive, our body is capable of transmitting messages that do not require much decoding. "The eyes have it, the eyes tell it, and the eyes know it," is a message that belongs not

in an optometrist's office but on a marriage counselor's wall,
for several women have mentioned that they can detect a
little twinkle in a man's eyes when he is interested in going
beyond the superficial level to a more intimate relationship.
The eyes have also been described as the window to the
brain, so be aware that your eyes may be signaling interest
and desire long before the other parts of your body catch
up. At a party, if your eyes are dancing to every available
person in the room, you may be communicating something
you'll wish you'd never said.

Another important tip-off was suggested to me by
former UCLA counselor Joan Rose, who said, "People who
are not looking and not sending off messages are not hustled.
It's as simple as that." If you find that men or women are
always trying to make passes at you at parties or at work,
examine your own body language and behavior. You are
probably sending out signals either consciously or unconsciously that communicate "Hi, I'm available." Said a woman
I know, "I knew my marriage was in trouble when I found
myself always dressing for someone else. My husband and I
would be getting ready, and my mind was always on my wardrobe as a way to communicate my availability to other men."

In addition, how you touch or embrace a friend of the
opposite sex may help you come to an understanding of the
intimacy of that relationship. Is the goodbye embrace after
a party really a hello for the next time? Is the arm around
the waist a symbol of love and friendship, or is it intended to
be something more? The body often knows the answer before
the mind, so stop, look, and listen to what it is telling you.

9. *Are you weakening your defenses against an affair by
the use of a mind-altering substance, such as alcohol or marijuana?* In a close extramarital friendship, your final ounce of
resolve may be dissolved by a bottle of wine, a gin and tonic,
or a joint of marijuana. If you allow these substances to decrease your inhibitions while heightening your sexual desire,
you may be making yourself more vulnerable to the start of an

affair you really might not want on sober reflection. So ask yourself, has your pattern of drinking changed to enable you to feel freer at parties, less inhibited and more comfortable with the opposite sex? Do you feel you need to get a slight "buzz on" to enjoy social occasions? If the answer is yes, be careful, because alcohol and affairs mix. Know the power of alcohol, appreciate its ability to change mood and behavior, and avoid combining it with the private time you spend with a special friend.

Tip-Offs in Your Spouse's Behavior

The more aware you are of your own behavior as it relates to a potential affair, the more sensitive you will be in judging your spouse's behavior. As I know from my own experience (as I wrote in chapter 1), I began to recognize in my wife behavior I myself had experienced, and I was able to confront her directly with my suspicions. This began the process that defused our potential affairs. However, as I talk here about tip-offs to your spouse's possible affair, I am certainly not advocating CIA-type activity or paranoia, where each little behavior change or warning signal is viewed as a cause for great alarm. *Unwarranted and unjustified suspicion or confrontation may be hazardous to the health of your marriage*. At the same time though, naive, head-in-the-sand behavior on your part may be as potentially dangerous. Therefore, an honest look at unusual behavior may help in the ultimate prevention of an affair.

"I was remodeling a kitchen in Beverly Hills," began a carpenter who was doing cabinet work in our home, "and the wife seemed to be a pretty square lady—a button-up-to-the-neck type. But after her husband left for work every morning, she would go upstairs and change clothes. She would put on a see-through blouse without a bra and then hang around us all day, talking and trying to turn us on. Once she even said, 'I'm going to take a shower now so don't walk in on me.' I'm pretty square myself, but that sounded like an invitation to me." If this woman's husband could have seen that scenario on videotape, he would have quickly realized that his wife was looking for an affair, or at least a fling. Perhaps he already knew, but this blatant tip-off could have triggered an awareness of his marriage's shortcomings, and professional help might have been sought.

The signals are rarely given so clearly by a spouse who is contemplating or activating an affair. Men and women may be obvious in advertising their availability, but usually affairs themselves are signaled by more subtle signs and only in retrospect do they seem obvious to the innocent spouse. Some of the tip-offs are the familiar ingredients of soap opera dramas: a sudden rash of late nights at the office, perfunctory performance of responsibilities at home or in the bedroom, and total indifference to the married partner's world. Said one woman whose husband had had a series of brief affairs before she finally had had enough and sought a divorce, "I've talked with some friends and they agree with me that you can generally sense when your spouse is having an affair or is close to it. You sense it by the formal manner in which he relates to you. You can almost spot when something is going on underneath and it's not being expressed." A follow-up piece of advice that I've learned from the people who have come to me for counseling is that when a spouse says "It's none of your business," it probably is.

Behavior and personality changes are indispensable to the vitality of our marriages. Therefore, it is safe to assume that none of the following five changes—if seen in your spouse—will necessarily signal an affair. However, if you believe, as I do, that human beings usually telegraph impending major changes, it is understandable that one or all of these changes may be present prior to an affair. These tip-offs were provided by a thirty-eight-year-old mother of four who said she noticed them in herself before her affair.

1. "I changed my style of dress. Loose-fitting blouses and

designer jeans replaced monogrammed sweaters and wrap-around skirts. My hair and its style became important to me, and I kept the style current. My total look was new and younger."

2. "My old friends were still important, but they lacked the vitality and breadth of interest that I now expected. I was tired of talking about children, husbands, volunteering, and the women in the neighborhood; I started putting down all that I had been a part of for so many years."

3. "My demands for equal time away from home with my new friends became all-consuming. I certainly saw no reason why I had to account for my time or activities; my husband never did, so why should I?"

4. "I asked for and got a release from always going to the family cabin for our summer vacation. I wanted time in the winter to go skiing or to Club Med. That is where all the action is."

5. "Talking about sex became a newfound pastime. Little offhand comments and sexual innuendos were commonplace, and when anyone opened the way to a sexual conversation, I was a willing participant."

Confrontation

One Thanksgiving morning the phone rang just as I was leaving the house to officiate at a special worship service. "Peter, I need to talk to you now," shouted Stan. "I just have to see you." I asked him to meet me at my office at 10:40, and when I arrived he was already there, pacing back and forth.

"I took my wife out to dinner last night," he began, "just the two of us, and she proceeds to tell me about this jerk she's been seeing who she thinks she likes, loves . . . whatever. She flat out told me she wants to have an affair. Can you believe that? I lost my appetite pretty quick. I've also lost all respect for her."

I listened to Stan's monologue for about twenty minutes, waiting for him to calm down, but realizing that the best counsel I could give him at that moment was to be a good listener and a supportive friend. Not until later did we begin to examine his marriage to see *why* his wife wanted the affair.

The confrontation by Stan's wife points up two different philosophies about whether or not to confront your partner with feelings you have for someone else—especially before there has been sex.

One philosophy is expressed by Dr. Anthony Rosenthal, Associate Clinical Professor of Psychiatry at the University of Southern California. He feels that direct expression of one's feelings may in fact be an indirect way of expressing aggression. "If you tell your spouse, 'I'm really turned on to somebody else,' the message may be that you find the other person more attractive and interesting than your spouse. It may be more accurate to say, 'I'm feeling unappreciated and neglected and let's talk about it.'"

This view is shared by many other professionals as well as nonprofessionals and was clearly articulated by Jill, a thirty-seven-year-old mother of three small children and a fashion coordinator. "Direct honesty can become brutal honesty," she said, "and a lot of women don't want to hear the fact that their husband was having an affair. I wouldn't even want to hear that he was *thinking* about having one. He can tell me that he thinks there are things wrong with our marriage and that we need to work on it, but I don't want him to go into details about how he is feeling about his secretary or some other women."

The alternative method of confrontation is to first question your own behavior and to then openly share these feelings—whatever they might be—with your spouse. I feel that this ability to "come clean" with yourself and to level with your spouse is an important method of partner interaction, but I offer three key warnings:

1. Proceed with caution and show a concern for your

spouse's feelings, for many people cannot handle direct honesty when it involves a rival outside the marriage.

2. Your express purpose should be to try to illuminate the difficulties you see in the marriage. If you are out to hurt your spouse or to even the score for perceived injustices, then confrontation is clearly unhealthy and counterproductive.

3. Be willing to accept and work through the consequences when you "get the cards on the table." The marriage now has to be played out, even if it becomes a verbal battlefield.

Most counselors advise against the "get-everything-off-your-chest" style of confrontation, arguing that too often the marriage is irreparably damaged over the issue of infidelity. I respect this point of view and I too urge individuals to err on the side of caution, sensitivity, and selectivity. Still, the question remains: What to do with suspicion about your own feelings for another person or the extramarital behavior of your spouse? As the guilty party do you tell your spouse? As the innocent party do you confront your spouse?

For both questions there is an analogy that might be helpful. Perhaps what is happening in your life or your spouse's life is analogous to a plane's going down a runway before takeoff. There is a point of no return when the pilot must take off; he cannot abort the flight because the commitment has been made. There is often such a point in an extramarital relationship, and this is why *I prefer to have people err on the side of early honesty and confrontation.* When you share your feelings with your spouse about another person before you go to bed with that person or you encourage your spouse to share similar feelings, the issue of a dysfunctional marriage will generally come out in the open before a divorce appears inevitable. After you have become involved with another person in a sexual relationship, trying to level with your spouse about the feelings you have can prove extremely damaging and hurtful, even to the strongest of individuals.

To many counselors, the issue is not whether there should be confrontation, but rather the *how* of confrontation. For example, if you have a strong gut feeling that your spouse is cheating on you, suggest that you go together to see a counselor who can ease you through the difficult situation of confrontation. Without condemning your spouse or assuming guilt unfairly, you can explain why his or her behavior has been confusing and disappointing to you; rather than point an accusing finger, you can express feelings that are chewing you up inside. By sharing your feelings, you bring the issue out in the open, and this leaves room for your partner to respond to you.

On the other hand, if you are beginning to drift from your marriage and toward someone else, it may be helpful to diffuse the issue by confessing these strong feelings that you have. For example, you might broach the subject by saying, "I'm falling for somebody at work and I haven't cheated on you yet, but we need to talk about it because I'm losing perspective on our marriage." In doing so, you are likely to begin a process of disclosure that has been lacking in your marriage for years. Opening up dialogue with one's spouse before going to bed with another person has short-circuited many affairs—and it could help save your marriage.

CHAPTER 11

Practical Principles for Marriage

Affair-prevention techniques are obviously important, but the best defense begins with the marriage itself. Books abound on the subject of how to nurture a healthy marriage, so my concern in this chapter will be to simply present some of my favorite approaches. These practical guidelines can strengthen your marriage relationship and diminish the appeal of an affair, but remember: instant solutions are hard to find, and it takes time and effort to implement changes.

Spouse Numero Uno

"Peter," began my dad, "I want you and your brother, Jay, to realize an important fact about the Kreitler family. Your mother is number one. She came first, and she will always be first. You guys are important, but Mom is number one." End of lecture—but darn good fatherly counsel and sage wisdom to pass on to others.

Who or what is number one in your life? You? Your kids? Your spouse? Your job? Your hobby? A lot of attention is given to the theory that you alone are number one and that the preservation of that ranking is crucial to your well-being. But this hypothesis troubles me, because I've found that some affairs are, in part, the result of being so focused on one's own happiness that there's no desire to work on the marriage. Granted, we are ultimately responsible only to ourselves, but I am convinced that living for others (and putting others first) is the only way we find meaning in our lives.

Placing and keeping our spouse numero uno is a difficult task. We all live in a world that pushes us to gain success, power, money—often at the expense of our close family relationships. Keeping people number one is hard; keeping our spouse number one is even harder. How easy it is to slide into an easy acceptance of our spouse and to gradually diminish his or her No. 1 status, which we proclaimed on our wedding day. One housewife was bluntly honest when she admitted that her husband was now number four on her list. First came her mom, who was ill and in a nursing home in the next town. Second were her two children, age nine and twelve. Third were all the parents and school kids, because she was active in the PTA. And fourth was her husband. Making her husband number four meant that what should have been her primary object of affection, love, and attention was relegated to a second-class status. I warned her that if her husband was left in this position for very long, he would eventually seek someone who made him numero uno.

Certainly there are times in your marriage when the pressing needs of family, children, and work must and do come first. But, if you can reassure your spouse that this is a temporary situation and that he or she is still No. 1, you may alleviate misunderstandings and a reason for wandering from the nest. Affirm your priorities regularly and don't confuse them, for a spouse who feels like No. 1 will in turn treat you like No. 1.

The Most Important Room

Imagine for a moment the perfect spot for making love and sleeping with your spouse. The space will probably not be an ordinary room with four walls, a lamp, a bedside table, a TV, two dressers, a book rack, and a clock radio. It will have something that makes it unique: windows to the mountains or ocean, dimmed lights and soft music, satin sheets on a gigantic bed, a glowing fireplace. In other words, in our imagination this perfect spot is a place of celebration and joy, a romantic hideaway.

Does your bedroom reflect this mood you've created in your fantasy? Mundane as your room may appear (with perhaps a view toward the next-door-neighbor's kitchen), it can create this feeling, and it can be a place to which you want to return again and again—if you make it the most important room in your house or your apartment. I view the bedroom as a symbolic place set aside for clearly defined reasons—to sleep and to make love. We can do what we do there in other places, but the bedroom and its bed are an outward and visible sign of something inward and personal taking place between two people. Create a bedroom atmosphere that is inviting, and special things begin to happen within that space. Desanctify the bedroom and you will diminish the chances of making sleep and lovemaking special.

Do you enjoy your bedroom? Is it set aside for a special purpose in your marriage, or have you made it a catch-all room for the house? The bedroom should not be a den, a TV room, a storage area, a playroom for the baby, nor a place to argue and fight. Of course, it is all of these things at times, but your goal should be to have it remain a haven where two people can celebrate their love in the most intimate and personal way possible.

I'm also an advocate of couples' sleeping together in the same bed whenever possible, for what happens in sleep itself often signals a relationship that is close or perfunctory. A special communication exists between two people when they cuddle and remain close in their sleep; that moving-about experience, where arms and night clothes get tangled, sheets get all askew, and bodies bump in profound and delightful moments of love, reflects the best interaction possible.

One of the women in Linda Wolfe's book *Playing Around* told how she appreciated the fact that her husband wasn't bored with her either sexually or in other ways; "in fact," she conceded, "he is even fun to sleep with. I mean sleep, and that is terribly important. He's affectionate in his sleep. He makes me feel that he really knows I'm there and that he appreciates my presence."

Apparently when a couple is asleep together, they often reach a level of awareness characterized by deep relaxation that ensures a refreshing interchange. Dr. Richard Klemer, in his book *Counseling in Marital and Sexual Problems*, talked about this aspect of sleep in beautiful terms: "I have come to respect the role of touch and body contact during sleep in enriching a marriage. Perhaps one partner awakens in the night to find his body moving rhythmically in response to the movements of the other, in an act of love so spontaneous, so unplanned as to seem without any conscious direction. Such episodes as these are almost unforgettable."

You and your spouse will spend perhaps a third of your married life in your bedroom, so how you approach this room—the attitude you have about it—will play an important role in affair prevention. One simple step involves trying to go to bed at the same time; it is difficult to enjoy the full pleasures of sleep together if one partner goes to bed at 10:00 and the other crawls in at 11:30. Also, you might rethink the bed itself—is it too large, too small, or too uncomfortable to ensure the kind of sleep I'm talking about? God knew what he was doing when he created man and woman needing sleep to refresh and vitalize. And sleep can do the same for your marriage.

Menninger Time

The idea of consciously setting aside time to be together would have been laughed at by the rural farm families of a generation ago. But today, the busy modern family needs to

schedule time for family interaction—not just for the parents
and the children but for husband and wife. Daily routines
designed to build family and marital unity, trust, and understanding are necessary in a world that allows so little time
for these rituals.

In your own marriage, you require—and should insist
on—designated time to talk with your spouse just to touch
base: to rehash the day's mini-drama and to discuss concerns
about the kids, finances, in-laws coming to visit, or an impending trip. This can be a time to air negative and positive
feelings, but it shouldn't be seen as or turned into a daily
gripe session. This is a time when you can renegotiate the
little contracts in your marriage and when impending tension or anger can be diffused constructively.

Dr. Will Menninger, the late president of the Menninger Foundation in Topeka, Kansas, and his wife, Cay, set
aside time from 10:30 to 11:00 every night. They maintained
this ritual for years, and it was so vital to their personal life
that it became known as Menninger Time. The success of
their marriage was well noted by local Topekans, and the
word spread that it was due in part to Menninger Time.

You and your spouse may want to arrange this special
time at the beginning of the day, depending upon your
schedules. While on a trip to Mexico, I met a young couple,
Steve and Sherri Collins, who told me they set aside time
every morning of the week before they head off for work.
The television is off and the newspaper is pushed away, and
they just talk for thirty minutes—"about most anything,"
said Sherri. "When we 'get tight' with each other, the whole
day goes better. If we begin the day with anger or we're late
for work and we don't get that time together, it affects our
attitude the rest of the day. So we try not to let anything
take priority over that thirty minutes."

Whenever this time comes, make it an integral part of
your daily life, for in doing so you will make those quiet,
reflective times with other people seem less intriguing.

Synchronize Watches

Practically every marriage can take heed from this insight given by an advertising account executive. "We were like two ships passing in the night," he said. "Whenever my wife had time for me, I didn't have time for her and vice versa. Gradually it worked out that we never made time to do anything together, and when we finally realized what was happening, it was too late; she was spending time with her boyfriend, and I was involved with my sail boat. We grew apart because we mismanaged the free time we did have."

Nearly all of us who are married live busy, committed lives, with time a commodity that seems to be increasingly controlled by someone or something else, due to the many demands on our lives and our involvement outside the marriage. Certainly some of these time restraints have to be accepted, but we can benefit from the example given us by those having affairs. Couples in love go to great lengths to make every moment count. They know the value of keeping their watches synchronized to ensure shared time. Planning rendezvous, avoiding detection, calling when "the coast is clear," and arranging the chance encounters all involve a serious consideration of the clock. Their time together is well orchestrated ("I'll call at 9:05, after I'm at the office and your kids have left for school"), and as a rule, they do not keep each other waiting; many a red light has been run or an appointment postponed so the appointment of the day can be kept with your lover.

You, too, can make the same kind of deliberate efforts to gain time with your spouse. Synchronize your watches by arranging lunches together, calling at specified times just to talk about how the day is going, or marking off weekends on the calendar and refusing to allow anything to take precedence over that time. A friend made this comment about his wife,

"Donna is good at planning little events. She sees boredom coming, and she plans something we can do alone or with friends."

If you and your spouse function on different schedules, and many couples experience this, try to understand and accept the differences—but pledge to compromise until both of you are satisfied. Do not let your lives grow apart like one couple I know, where the seldom-happy wife complained to me, "I'm a night person and he's a day person. On weekends I want to stay up and party, but he bags it early so he can get up at 5:30 and run his damn eight miles." When married partners allow their lives to pass in the night like this— when they become "single marrieds" (living single lives but being married)—passage will eventually be booked with a person whose watch is in sync and who will make time for you.

Know Your Energy Limitations

Each of us has a definable limit to our physical abilities. We know whether we are capable of hitting a golf ball 250 yards, running a marathon in three hours, lifting a 100-pound bag of fertilizer, or catching our little leaguer's fast ball. For our body's sake, it is important to ascertain and then accept these defined limits. Yet it is more difficult and equally crucial to be aware of the limitations of our emotional energy and how they can affect our marriage.

I learned a good lesson early in my marriage. I had been struggling through the first two years of seminary because the commitment to the ministry was a difficult decision for me to make. In addition to the daily routine of academia, I had trouble allaying my mental anguish, and I never seemed to have time or energy for the number one person in my life—my wife. Even our bedroom became a study hall. Finally one day, in a fit of justifiable anger, Edon swept my books off the bed as she shouted, "Damn seminary and damn books." For too long I had been bringing the office home, and she had reached the end of her rope. That cleared the air and gave me the jolt I needed to bring a more sensible perspective to what I was doing to our marriage.

In your own marriage, how often do you arrive at the end of the day emotionally drained—either from your job or from having to manage the household? It happens too often to all of us, men and women alike, because we tend to get absorbed in our own daily routines. As a result, we have nothing or very little left over for the most important people in our lives—our spouse and our kids. Most everyone hates a steady diet of leftovers. When that is all there is in the refrigerator, the appeal to go out to dinner is very strong. Similarly, if all we have to greet us at the end of the day is a "left over" partner, and this pattern exists day after day, we may be inclined to go elsewhere to find someone who has energy for us. (As I'll point out in chapter 12, one reason affairs have such an appeal is that they tend to be sustained in the daytime, when both lovers are alert, awake, and energized.)

Certainly there are going to be days when you or your spouse are legitimately drained because of inordinate pressures or demands. But my experience tells me that these times of complete "wash out" can be minimized to a great extent when precautions are taken.

One method is to try to get a handle on what absorbs your mental energies during the day, whether it's pressure, tension, deadlines, appointments, fear of your boss, demands by your children, or anxiety about family or financial problems. Whatever the source of that energy loss, seek to isolate it so that it does not carry over and infect your relationships at home. This is difficult to do, I know, but recognize that your energy drain is something independent of your spouse and avoid using him or her as your target. Instead, try to burn off tension with an exercise break or rekindle your spirit by taking a cat nap or by setting aside ten minutes for prayer or meditation. Do all you can to ensure that you have something left for your life at home at night.

Vacation as Recreation and Re-Creation

"I work so I can play" is perhaps the most common philosophy of life espoused today by Americans. We are a nation constantly in pursuit of new and better leisure-time activities, helped along by jobs that are giving us increasing time for vacations and three-day weekends. One of our largest industries, in fact, is the support of those people who are on vacation. So it behooves us, as married couples, to take a special look at our vacations in terms of how they can help us build our defenses against affairs.

A good vacation can revitalize your marriage in several ways, if you plan and use that time wisely. In the traditional sense, couples need to get away periodically (with or without children) just for relaxation, recreation, and a broadening of experience. Vacations give us a chance to vacate a familiar environment—our home, neighborhood, and office—so we can travel to a new place to be refreshed, renewed, and invigorated. Unwinding like this from the rigors and predictability of our daily routines can aid our communication, sex lives, relations with the kids, and personal well-being.

Yet for many couples, vacation time is frantic time: packing and unpacking bags, hustling in and out of hotels, motels, and restaurants so that as many new places, sights, and activities as possible can be included. Leisure-time activities may be included, but *invariably little time on vacation is set aside for re-creation of the marriage.* Out of all this comes a typical frustration, as reflected by the response of a tired, hard-working father who told me, "You know, for years I've been going off on vacations with my wife and kids to resorts and summer houses, and every year the last three or four days are agony; I can't wait to get back to work. The kids get on my nerves, I can't take my wife twenty-four hours a day, and I get bored with the day-to-day routine that is expected of me—the tennis, swimming, hiking, drinking, barbeques. I can never really relax and recharge my batteries." Vacation for this man has been work transferred to a different place with a different set of activities, but still with that sense of obligation to do this and to do that.

If your sentiments are reflected here, then you should look closely at why you go on a vacation in the first place. If the sole purpose is to play, then the chances are good that vacations will never live up to your expectations. But if you can go away with the purpose of strengthening and renewing the ties to your spouse (and your children), the by-product might be a lot of play time and good fun—as well as greater personal and marital happiness. It is precious time that can lead to positive growth.

Once, while waiting for a flight at Los Angeles airport, I struck up a conversation with Robert Bassett and his wife, who were returning home to Canada after a three-week holiday. They were enthusiastic about their travels around Southern California, but what they enjoyed best was their time for each other. They saw their vacation as an opportunity for re-creation, and they said that on the plane flight home they planned to evaluate what the trip had meant to their marriage.

This is a crucial point if you hope to have your vacation bring new life to your marriage once you return home. I have found that couples need to incorporate some form of evaluation into their vacation by debriefing the experience in terms of what it means to their marriage. When you take time to do this as you go along and after the vacation, you will frequently realize that your sex life was freer, more consistent, and more pleasurable (unless you were camping with the kids or sharing motel rooms). Also, communication channels are often more open on vacations because you are more relaxed and have more energy for thoughtful conversations. These positives of a vacation should be noted and recorded. Then you and your spouse may have a better chance facing reality once you return to your regular routine. Can you take what you have learned about each other and the marriage and bring this home? Or must you leave the good times back at the cabin in the woods or at the beach?

When possible, try also to plan short vacations or weekend trips away from home without the kids, even if you simply stay at a hotel in town. Such getaways can afford your marriage the luxury of "you and me" time, which is so hard to come by during the normal week-to-week activities. Morris Samuels, a counselor and priest, advises his clients to spend at least one weekend every six months away from everyone—family, friends, pets, chores, and responsibilities. Setting aside high-quality time like this, where you and your spouse can center on each other, is the most simple technique I know of for disarming potential "other-centered" relationships.

Water as a Prevention Aid

Common everyday situations are often overlooked in our serious attention to issues such as communication, managing time together, and the "ness" needs. Yet over the years I've noticed that an almost universal ingredient in affairs is the mutual enjoyment of water in its different settings. Out of this realization comes my conviction that we should value water not simply for the way it relaxes and refreshes, but for its romantically therapeutic quality inside our marriages. We know that couples having an affair often turn the practical arenas for bathing and relaxation and recreation into a place for sex. Yet several married couples I know bathe or shower together regularly, not with sex consciously in mind but to discover the joy of water, dialogue, touching, and closeness all in ten or fifteen minutes a day. As they wash each other with soap, they also wash away any anger or tension felt toward each other. These shared showers are moments of touching and intimacy that are remembered during the day, and a celebration of love that need not be envied by lovers outside marriage.

Add Romance

A good friend recently arranged a dinner party in honor of his wife's thirty-fifth birthday and invited four other couples. On the day of the dinner the host purchased five crystal bud vases at a gift shop and then five long-stem red roses at a florist. When the guests gathered at the restaurant, each lady found a special, unexpected gift at her place. One woman, obviously pleased, turned to the host and exclaimed, "I didn't know you had such a romantic instinct."

We all have the capacity to keep romance alive in our marriages by adding the little touches that we used to dream up during our courting years—and which always mean a great deal to wives and husbands alike, no matter how long they've been married. Yet too often we choose not to take the time or make the extra effort that is needed. So think ahead and plan special moments. For example, a personal gift usually takes on more meaning than the actual value of the gift. "When you're caught up in a love affair," commented a woman who was falling in love again, "you will spend five or ten dollars on something absolutely worthless in its intrinsic value, but it means much more than that to the relationship." Therefore, be selective in choosing the appropriate gift for your spouse, since the choice can indeed speak as loud as love language.

Romance in a marriage can also make the commonplace a little different and hence more appealing. A woman who has been married thirty-five years said that she still works hard keeping romance alive—"Even if I have to serve hamburgers and french fries by candlelight, with a nice bottle of wine." Meanwhile, a wise husband will do his part to warm the marriage by not only setting a crackling fire in the fireplace, but by putting on his wife's favorite background music.

We know that affairs are nourished by romance: they feed off candlelight, moonlight, the well-chosen restaurant, the colorful bouquet of flowers. So think of similar ways to freshen up your marriage and you will share an outward and visible sign of something felt inside—the love you have for your spouse.

The Value of Laughter

Recently a woman came to me to talk about why her marriage had failed. Her husband had abruptly left home because of his infatuation with a younger, livelier woman. The wife told me that as she reflected on her marriage, she realized she could not remember the last time she had laughed with her husband—or heard him laugh around the house. She recognized, too, that she had helped bring about that situation by taking everything too seriously and by not creating an atmosphere at home where laughter could germinate and grow and be expressed.

When was the last time you and your spouse had a good laugh together? This may not seem important, but laughter between two people is a cherished part of successful relationships—and easily overlooked in many marriages today. Sol Gordon, Director of the Institute for Family Research and Education at Syracuse University, drew up a list of key ingredients in marriage, and in order of importance, he listed laughter first (followed by friendship, involvement, sex, sharing, integrity, talk, love, adaptability, and tolerance).

Laughter fosters intimacy and encourages touch and communication. Reflect back to your early days of dating and you may recall that one of the first signs of attraction to another was the ability to effortlessly laugh together. The cause of the laughter may have been inane, but it was spontaneous and meaningful—a bridge to more openness and honesty.

Kids laugh all the time, lovers laugh, but married people too often forget how to laugh, and this everything-is-so-serious approach to life may ultimately threaten the marriage.

There is much genuine humor in marriage, so make sure you allow it a chance to breathe; recognize the humorous side, not the bleak side, of events that occur everyday. Don't take yourself too seriously—be quick to laugh—and you'll be fun to be with, as a person and as a married partner.

Let the Child Out

I have found that one of the major reasons why people are so enamored by the idea of an affair is they long for plain, old-fashioned Disneyland fun amidst their world of responsibilities, commitments, and deadlines. They see the frolicking, playful side of life come alive in the interaction between lovers, and they yearn to have the same experience.

How does your marriage measure up? Has the fun gone out of the relationship? Are you so wrapped up in the stifling cocoon of being an adult that you have lost the innate freedom we all have to be young again: to run and holler on the beach, to delight in building sand castles or snowmen, to jump into a pile of leaves, to ride merry-go-rounds, to fly kites, or to throw snowballs? *In short, are you a big kid at heart and not afraid to reveal that fact?* Do you let the spirited, child-like side of your personality have its place in your marriage—and do you encourage the same behavior by your spouse? A good example is that party situation we have all experienced where the husband, in some goofy but natural way, is entertaining to everybody but his wife, whose face reveals her discomfort at what she considers to be ridiculous behavior.

If you realize that you rarely have spontaneous, effortless fun in your marriage, there is really nothing holding you back. Who knows, when you let the child in you emerge—out into the open and not with a lover—something magical may happen between you and your spouse. You may re-awaken and rejuvenate old behavior patterns that you found so appealing before you were married.

Take Time to Be Still

When something begins to happen to your feelings toward another person, one of the most important qualities you can possess is the ability to take time to listen to yourself think. Stop-look-listen is a warning sign that will prevent collisions with powerful locomotives, and listening for that "still small voice" inside you—that inner recorder—may prevent a head-on collision with an affair.

In Robert Johnson's fascinating book, *She: Understanding Feminine Psychology,* he speaks of the woman as too often jumping into the middle of situations. Whereas, "She needs to be quiet, to approach the vastness of life's responsibilities in a more orderly manner, to do one thing, take one crystal goblet at a time, concentrate on it and do it well." The married man, in a similar way, should learn to focus on what Kansas City psychiatrist Dr. John O'Hearne calls the "island quality." When under stress, he should center in on himself by visualizing himself alone on an island: a unique individual, solitary, peaceful, set apart, and not bothered by the rest of the world as he makes his important decisions.

We love to lead with our heart in interpersonal relationships, but at critical times we need to step back and lead with the head. This was the approach taken by a married woman I know who, after wrestling long and hard with the pro's and con's of having an affair, finally decided that the cost would be too great. She told me that her decision boiled down to listening to either her head or her heart. "My heart kept saying 'yes, yes, yes' and my head 'no, no, no.' I finally stepped back from my relationship to both men and I took time to listen. I thought about my children and the article I had read in *Newsweek*, 'Children of Divorce,' and I realized there was too much at stake to gamble on an affair."

The Marital Checkup

One of the most common reasons given for why a marriage fails is the time-honored excuse "We simply grew apart." This process does not just naturally happen but is the result of inattention to the marriage. There are a number of ways to prevent this drifting apart, but the tactic that makes the most sense to me is the marriage checkup, done once or twice a year.

The goal of such a checkup is to examine your marriage in terms of reinforcing what is good in it and repairing what is going wrong before it is too late. This can be accomplished with an objective third-party listener (e.g., the person who married you or a good listener in any of the helping professions) or by setting aside your own space and time to honestly appraise your marriage. I have even toyed with the idea of handing out a warranty card to every couple I marry, asking them (if they remain in the area) to come and visit me every six or twelve months just to talk about their marriage.

One reason I feel so strongly about such a checkup is that we tend to let difficult or distasteful problems in a marriage slide until it is too late to do anything constructive about them. A checkup invariably illuminates some weak spots that can be eliminated with a little work and attention. Such a forum can also encourage a spouse to raise festering but as yet unspoken dissatisfactions about the way the marriage is going. Moreover, when checkups are held yearly, they will naturally occur at those crucial times when affairs are common (for example, when a woman turns thirty and a man turns forty).

What might happen in a marital checkup? Each counselor's approach will differ, but I try to help people discover the Achilles' heel of their marriage while simultaneously reinforcing the positive aspects of their life together. Here are some questions that briefly probe some common areas of concern.

- How is the sexual relationship going? (I find that the *quality* of a couple's sex life—not necessarily the quantity —is an excellent barometer for measuring the overall emotional climate of the marriage.)
- Are each of you supportive and helpful of each other?
- Do you try to understand your partner's needs? Are you *aware* of his or her un-met needs?
- What are your priorities? Have they changed in recent months or years?
- What worries you about the marriage?
- Do you make time to communicate?
- Are each of you taking responsibility for your own lives? (This concept is basic to the whole book—the idea that you are ultimately responsible for your own affair prevention and therefore your own marital happiness. Are you taking steps to grow as a person? Are you interested in new activities, ideas, and goals? Are you broadening your horizons?)

A marital checkup may reveal major trouble in your marriage, just a couple of problem areas, or perhaps a relationship that is vibrantly healthy and happy. In whatever case, such a checkup might be the best fifty- to one-hundred-dollar-investment you can make in your marriage; not just in emotional terms but in dollars and cents, for unexamined "drifting" can lead to the need for extensive marriage counseling—or an expensive divorce.

All of us spend time and money maintaining our personal appearance and our wardrobe—the externals that we believe are so vital to our peace of mind and happiness. Spending time and money on the invisibles—the inner person—comes much harder, and it is so often neglected in marriage. But when you and your spouse commit yourselves to regular marital checkups, this signifies that you value each other enough to do whatever you can to affirm the worth of your marriage.

Communication and Conflict Resolution

In our search for directives that can help guarantee marital bliss and the maintenance of marital fidelity, the skills of communication and conflict resolution are as close to a concise prescription as I can find. When these two specific abilities are absent in a marriage, the potential greatly increases for one or both partners to seek a conflict-free relationship with good communication—and this often may mean an affair.

Much has been written about communication and its central place in the life of two people living together. Yet what is one of the common complaints of wives and husbands everywhere—especially after they've lived together for five, ten, or twenty-five years? "My spouse will just not sit down and talk with me. We never have time together to carry on a conversation about anything. I don't think he has really listened to what I have had to say in years." Or the dialogue might be this: "I wish I could get my husband to open up to you, Peter. He's going through a really tough time at work, but he won't talk to me about it. He holds everything to his chest. He must be letting it all out *someplace*—but where, and with whom?

Situations like this are common, and it may take time for you to break old patterns of not sharing words and feelings. If you are in a marriage that has a words-of-significance void, or you and your partner have never learned how to communicate, then a few simple thoughts may be of help. Establish a home environment that is conducive to communication among all members, especially husband and wife. Set aside a comfortable arena for dialogue—the dinner table (after the dishes have been cleared away), chairs around a coffee table, pillows in front of the fireplace—that is away from distractions as much as possible, especially the television. Then really try to listen to what your partner has to say. If you do not understand, ask questions. Buy a how-to book on communication and read it. Attend a seminar at your local college, university, church, or synagogue. Enroll in a Marriage Encounter weekend or a similar course that will aid in communication.

In relation to affair prevention, I feel there are two very clear reasons couples should know how to communicate:

First, good listeners are in short supply and great demand and once discovered they are sought as friends—or as lovers. Thus, communicating at home might obviate your spouse's need to always talk deeply with someone other than yourself. Feelings such as these might then disappear: "My husband spends more time talking to his secretary than he does me" or "My wife is always gabbing on the phone with her friends; she doesn't even hang up when I get home." If this sounds familiar, perhaps your inability to listen or your lack of interest in what your spouse has to say is contributing to his or her need to communicate so intensely elsewhere.

Second, communication is a necessary step toward conflict resolution. As Dr. Carlfred Broderick emphasized in *Human Sexuality*: "Perhaps the most important single preventive of adultery is a developed and well-oiled mechanism for dealing with strain in the marriage." As mentioned earlier, one of the appeals of an affair is that it presents itself as a conflict-free relationship (at least initially), which contrasts with the fact that a marrige is rarely conflict free for long periods of time. Therefore, the image of an affair beckons during periods of intense marital strain. Continual conflict and the inability to resolve the strains of marriage wear down even the staunchest advocates of marital fidelity.

There are several major conflicts common to nearly all marriages—over sex, money, how to raise and discipline the children, in-laws, the demands of a career, and so on—and the less obvious irritants, if left unresolved, often cause major tension and strain: unappealing personal hygiene, sloppiness, inattention to the chores that make a house a comfortable home, an obsession with one's exercise program or outside activities while a spouse's interests are given scant attention, and so on. These conflicts are natural in marriage, and avoiding them only enhances the tension; resolving them increases marital pleasure and decreases the presumed attraction of an affair. So a marriage that is always in the process of conflict resolution is a marriage that is becoming stronger, better, and more resilient to third-party involvement.

David Augsburger, in *Caring Enough to Confront*, offers five possible alternatives for a couple as they set about resolving either the petty or major strains in their relationship:

1. "I win—you lose." (The win-lose game is a dead-end street. Play it on a tennis court but not at home.)

2. "I want out—I'll withdraw." (The slam-the-door, I'm-escaping routine builds resentment and simply delays the problem to another day.)

3. "I'll give in for good relations." (This has limited life. Occasionally, capitulation may prevent a more difficult situation, but giving in decreases self-esteem and eventually produces self-defeat.)

4. "I'll meet you halfway." (This sounds like the ideal way to resolve conflicts. Compromise is vital in any marriage, and there are times when it makes good sense for each partner to sacrifice his or her position for the sake of the relationship. However, the situation is often resolved only temporarily and will reoccur in most cases.)

5. "I can care and confront."

We have all used some, if not all, of the above methods to try to resolve conflict at some point in our marriage. Mr. Augsburger offers the fifth alternative as the most loving and as offering the most potential for growth. I agree that it is perhaps the only effective deterrent to perpetual conflict. When there is a strain, confront it, because continual toleration of conflict in the marriage is a no-win situation, which may eventually drive you or your spouse to find a refuge from the storm—in the arms of someone who offers potential tranquility. Care enough to communicate the hurts and how the irritants are spoiling your peace of mind. They come with every relationship, and trying to run from them will merely perpetuate them.

In the marital blessing for the wedding service of the Episcopal church there is a phrase "May your home be a haven of blessing and peace." I feel that this is an ideal worth striving for, and you can help ensure that it happens by resolving the conflicts in your marriage along the way.

CHAPTER 12

Sexuality in Marriage

If you and your spouse are working toward an affair-proof marriage, then achieving a mutually satisfying sexual relationship must be given top priority. This may already be understood in your marriage, reflecting the comment by a woman in my congregation: "Sex is absolutely the greatest leveler there is. Everything can go wrong all day; your kids can be rotten, your husband can be rotten, but if the two of you can make love together, things can really smooth out." Yet perhaps you have stayed married for many years without having a good sexual relationship and your thinking is "We have a fine marriage, but sex is not that important to either of us; we don't really worry about it." I respect and accept that position, but it has been my counseling experience that healthy sex for both partners usually accompanies a satisfying marriage. Or as another woman in my congregation said, "If a man and woman are happy in bed, then there is no need to stray." Although people with good sex lives—as determined by their own standards—still stray from the nest, in most marriages a healthy sexual relationship greatly minimizes the temptation to explore extramarital sex.

Sex in marriage is a curious phenomenon. On the one hand, we have Andrew Greeley's statement that "our craving for sexual satisfaction, for sexual relief, for sexual union permeates our being and frequently dominates our behavior to the exclusion of all else." This point seems easy to confirm, given our national preoccupation with sex and all its permutations. However, this cultural pattern doesn't necessarily imply that couples give just as much attention to sex in the privacy of their marriage. On the contrary, I often find that sex between husband and wife is a relatively unimportant aspect of their life together—a once or twice a week (or month) encounter perhaps, with little or no discussion about their sexuality between these encounters. The innate sex drive people possess often finds its outlet in forms other than marital sexual union: in an affair, masturbation, reading or viewing pornography, or sublimated in one's job, family, or hobby.

Since we are all sexual beings—but with differing needs and priorities—I've prepared a number of guidelines that may, if needed, enhance the sexual relationship in your marriage, thereby diminishing the appeal of another person. The subject of sexuality is complex and highly subjective, and I do not pretend to be an expert, but over the years I've gathered advice and insights from many experts who have convinced me of the supreme value of married couples' having a mutually rewarding sexual experience.

Ensuring the Right Emotional Climate for Sex

When a couple works hard to ensure that the emotional climate in their marriage is conducive to sex, their lovemaking tends to occur easily and naturally. Setting the right mood—beforehand, during intercourse, and afterward—requires the effort of both partners and may necessitate altering long-accepted sexual patterns in their marriage. But when you and your spouse can eliminate the tension that often precludes sex from taking place (or that inhibits the enjoyment of one or both partners), change the routine, and show concern for each other's needs, then you'll begin to create—and sustain—an atmosphere in which sex can be warm, spontaneous, and fun . . . and something both of you look forward to. By not taking care to do this your sex life may erode, as typified by a working mother who told me she no longer enjoyed having sex with her husband, though they were only in their midthirties.

"He doesn't even try to turn me on," she lamented. "Sex used to be damn good for us, but all the spark is gone, and I now wonder if we can ever recapture the old feelings we once shared." Sue and Tony went to the same university and became pinned after their sophomore year. They never lived together, but many weekends were shared in his fraternity room, and sex was an accepted and natural part of their going steady. "Frankly, most of the fun was when we were in college," she recalled. "I can remember the kissing games, the touching, the fondling, the chasing, the undressing, the laughing. Now it's so mechanical and predictable. We get ready for bed about 10:00 or 10:30. I clean my teeth, take off my eye makeup, brush and put up my hair, do a few stretching exercises, put on my pajamas, and climb in bed. Meanwhile, Tony has gotten ready in a minute and a half and is sitting in bed watching the news. Usually, he offers to kiss me goodnight if he doesn't want any sex. If he does want sex, and he has been lying there thinking about it for twenty minutes, he's ready to go as soon as I climb in bed. I can't possibly gear up that fast. I'm just not emotionally equipped to 'turn on' like he can. Sometimes he will take time to get me ready physically—you know, with foreplay—and I'll do the same for him, but that only takes about a minute."

The pattern they had established was nonproductive and not very satisfying. I encouraged Sue and Tony to seek the counsel of a person skilled in communication and sexuality. They did, and they each realized that their ingrained habits precluded an adequate emotional climate for healthy sex, and the result was unsatisfying and infrequent sex. Together they became committed to recapture the old ways they had found so appealing during college.

Great lovers—men and women alike—are those who appreciate the *process* of loving; they take time to create the proper mood, enjoying the little steps along the way as their partner gets "turned on." Lovers savor those lingering moments at the beginning of sex, the slow buildup mixed with bursts of passion. "Why should married partners be in such a hurry?" asks Rona Lee Cohen, co-director of the Seminars on Sexuality in Los Angeles. "Faster sex certainly isn't better sex."

Skill at lovemaking does indeed take time and patience. In our world of instant everything, the "slam bam, thank you ma'am" style often takes precedence in bed. Too often, men concentrate on physical readiness, but they need to learn from women, many of whom emphasize repeatedly that *good sex has more to do with feelings than performance*; when a man or woman is emotionally prepared, the physical readiness will follow more easily. One woman spoke of her husband's ability to go from arousal to erection to intromission to orgasm to sleep in less than two minutes. He seemed to feel no guilt, and she was actually glad he could "get it over with that quickly," because sex was not fulfilling to her, and she could live without it—at least with her husband.

A number of therapists believe that many of the errors men make in lovemaking could be eliminated if they were simply more patient in their preparation for making love and more sensitive to that precious time of intimacy. "Men are so concerned about intercourse," admitted a counselee, Richard, "that they overlook the prelims to get to the main event. I've finally realized after all these years that when I do this with my wife—if I'm tired or too lazy or just want my release—it's an immediate turn-off, and she would just as soon forget it that night."

When lovers take time in the beginning and the middle of lovemaking, they tend to give time to the end. *In fact, for many couples those moments of touching, holding, cherishing, snuggling, and deep breathing after sex are often more pleasurable than the sex itself.* This time of closeness may last only a minute or two, but it brings a feeling of togetherness that is rarely duplicated elsewhere in the marriage. Many men and women have talked to me in glowing terms about the high quality of the time shared immediately after intercourse. The Reverend Morris Samuels told me that he affirms the value of his lovemaking with his wife by getting up, pouring a glass of sherry, climbing back in bed, sharing the drink, and then going to sleep.

Another way to enhance the post-sex experience is to offer thanks for the intimacy shared. Most people are quite comfortable offering thanksgiving for the blessings of good health, good fortune, food on the table, and good opportunities, but rarely does anyone see the value of offering thanks for the good sex that occurs within the marriage. So take a moment after sex to express your feelings of pleasure or appreciation, and the beginnings of sex will come more easily the next time.

Choosing to remember sex can also offer you and your spouse an unusual feedback of interesting dimensions. Those having affairs remember the good times of lovemaking and can recall in almost perfect detail its step-by-step process. They have a good memory of the event partly because it is new, exciting, and not too frequent. In contrast, married partners, when asked, rarely recall any of the specifics of touching—where they were touched, where it felt good—and what happened that made the event special. When you are able to retrieve the good experiences, you begin to ensure the continuation of satisfying sex with your spouse. And when you know what you want and can ask for it, you are taking a step toward a healthy sexual relationship.

Timing Your Sex Is Crucial

In a mature marriage, partners generally learn to defer gratification to a time when both of them can enjoy sex. They find their time, stick to it, and guard it well, for they know it is important to a good marriage. Try hard not to fall into a pattern of avoiding sex simply because you are too tired, but also be careful not to force sex when your partner has run out of energy. Fatigue is understandable among over-committed husbands and wives. At the end of the work day, after the kids have been put to bed, the kitchen cleaned, the laundry folded, the pets fed, the newspaper read, the bills paid, and the bedroom readied, mom and dad are often too tired to commit fifteen or thirty minutes to making love. So what to do to avoid that phrase heard in so many bedrooms: "Not tonight, honey; I'm too tired"?

One honest approach is taken by a couple I know who have been married for ten years, are parents of two young girls, and are both working and struggling to make mortgage payments on their suburban house. Dwight and Sandy literally fall into bed at night during the week, but what sets them apart from others in similar situations is that they have recognized their limitations. They have contracted to make few sexual demands, and they avoid forcing sex when it will be an obligation rather than a mutual desire. "We know we're going to be too tired during the week to enjoy sex," Sandy told me, "so we only make love on weekends. That is not rigid, but it has worked best that way."

"Are you happy with your sexual relationship?" I asked her. "Yes," she said. "I feel every time we have sex it is good sex; not always great, but always good because it is not forced. We both know when the time is appropriate. It is often Saturday mornings when the kids are watching TV. We are not tired, we can take our time, and our kids have learned to respect our right to have our door closed for what we call 'Mommy and Daddy's loving time.' "

Dwight and Sandy are realistic and discriminating, and their approach to sex works well for them. Another tip is offered us by those having affairs, who always seem to have unlimited energy for each other. Of course, they have an unfair advantage ("It's easy to be a mistress," one woman told me, "because you don't have Ajax on your hands"), but in their efforts to avoid detection, they often get together in the morning or over the lunch hour. This happens to coincide with our period of greatest available energy. Realistically, getting together alone with your spouse during midday hours may not be possible, but some creative thinking and planning could reveal numerous opportunities. One corporate executive I know, whose high-rise office building is just twenty-five minutes from home, began to take his wife to lunch once a week because he realized that he was more alert and more fun to be with at lunch than at dinner, when he was exhausted and the kids were around. At the end of their second lunch, the wife suggested they go home and make love before he returned to work, and this became a much-anticipated weekly event. Their high energy level in the early afternoon made the marriage blossom once again.

Timing is crucial to good sex and so is maintaining a regular pattern. Ultimately each couple must define for themselves how often it's best to have sex. What works best for you cannot be legislated by me or anyone else. But keeping sex regular has been shown to be of value in maintaining a healthy sexual relationship over the years and in making people feel good about themselves and their marriage. Infrequency of sex is considered by many therapists to be a dysfunction in the same category as impotence and frigidity. If having sex once a month is mutually satisfying to a couple, then who am I to judge that this is too frequent or infrequent? However, having sex every other month or even once a month may indicate that it does not have a high enough priority in the marriage, and counsel should be sought if this is of concern to either partner. Pay heed to the insight offered by Rona Lee Cohen, who said, "When there is no sex in marriage, there is no touching, and when there is no touching, there is no caring."

What is "regular"? Once a day, every other day, twice a week? My criterion is that what is regular to one spouse should be in fairly close harmony with the expectations and needs of the other spouse. This is something that should be clearly communicated, for as a delightful scene from the movie *Annie Hall* points out, a man and woman may share quite different perceptions about the same issue.

The movie screen showed two separate scenes, one of Annie with her analyst, the other of Woody Allen with his.

"How often do you have sex?" queried Annie's therapist.

"Oh, all the time," replied Annie. "Probably three times a week."

"How often do you have sex?" asked Woody's doctor.

"Oh, hardly at all," answered Woody. "Probably three times a week."

Bring Creativity and Variety to Your Sex Life

People are not biologically determined to be faithful or unfaithful, but if a couple expects fidelity, it is wise to sustain a sexual relationship that keeps encouraging newness, diversity, creativity, and adventure. "Variety seems to be a fundamental part of human sexual nature," writes Father Greeley, "and if one does not find it in the marriage bed—or in whatever substitute fantasy one may devise—one will be under strong pressure to look for it elsewhere." We are all well aware that for many people the tantalizing appeal of an affair is the presumed sexual adventures that will come with a different partner. This person is perceived as offering new sex and better sex and is therefore judged to be of more value in bed than one's partner.

The problem of sexual boredom in marriage was pointed out by an editor of *U.S. Catholic* magazine, who estimated that "it is safe to say the average, healthy married couple will have

intercourse upwards of 5,000 times during their marriage."
But, he added on a gloomy downbeat, "there are very few
people around who can do anything 5,000 times without
getting a bit bored with it."

Instead of letting your lovemaking habits slide into a
rut, put your God-given gift of imagination and creativity to
work in your bedroom. I'm not talking about sexual gymnastics or mate-swapping or open-sex retreats. What I am talking
about is taking the time to pursue diverse, enriching sexual
practices within your marriage. Discover for yourselves styles
of sexual pleasuring that are preferable above all others. Different positions can be tried. Books, seminars, and counselors
can be consulted for healthy alternatives to the common and
trusted patterns. Advises Los Angeles psychiatrist Anthony
Rosenthal, "Try to rekindle dying fantasies. If you do not
nourish them in the marriage, they may find expression elsewhere."

Variety, however, is more than technique—it is also
atmosphere and attitude, a willingness to try new lovemaking
arenas. I like the vignette offered by a woman who took a
unique approach to her husband's fortieth birthday. He arrived home at the end of the day in typical fashion—only this
time he was met at the door by his wife, who was carrying a
suitcase and a picnic kit. The baby-sitter had the children
seated at the table and out the door the wife and husband
went. "Happy Birthday, dear," she told him as they got in the
car. "We're going to an X-rated motel. I have everything. I
packed a supper for us; I have two bottles of wine, my night-
gown, and I'm ready." Their celebration was private, unique,
creative, and only $19.95 for three hours. Not only was this
a special evening of shared sexual pleasure, but it was also a
symbol of their mutual trust and openness and their belief
that a good sexual relationship was important to their marriage.

When you and your spouse are interested in creative

sexual experiences in your marriage and you couple this with years of shared history, the sexual pleasure that results can make an affair seem second rate at best. A thirty-seven-year-old mother of two who is very committed to her church, spoke of the positive value of a long sexual history with her spouse when she told me: "Sex has become a real sharing of ourselves. We have been married fifteen years, and sex is something different today; it is almost metaphysical. Sex like what we have now you could not get by changing partners over and over."

Enjoy Sex

Even in today's age of sexual liberation and enlightenment, some people still feel they must be given permission to engage in sex solely for its recreational value. My point to them is that sex should be enjoyed within their marriage, whatever the purpose or circumstances. God created us in such a fashion that the method by which we propagate our species is supremely pleasurable—from foreplay through afterplay. Here again we can learn from men and women who have affairs. Lovers are not out to make babies; they value sex for the intimacy, the touch, and the fun that is involved.

This does not mean that sex should be seen as a frivolous pursuit. As Masters and Johnson remind us, you cannot have good sex on a regular basis without commitment. Good sex is a subjective matter, but I equate the term with healthy sex—sex that is nonexploitive and produces self-esteem, pleasure, and mutual gratification without producing guilt. If this characterizes the sex you experience with your spouse, then you probably enjoy good sex. If so, cherish it, nourish it, and work hard to maintain that level of sharing—you are indeed fortunate.

Talk About Sex with Your Spouse

When I encourage people to give sex a high priority in their marriage, I also mean giving the subject air time. Your sex life together should be talked about as much as it is done—in an open, nonjudgmental, nonthreatening manner. Some people feel "Do it—don't talk about it," but sex is a part of every adult's life, and the chances are excellent that sex is read about, thought about, and discussed someplace or with someone by every married person. When you introduce sexual dialogue at home—in bed or elsewhere—you take a big step toward having a satisfying, productive marriage.

The problem is that relatively few couples regularly sit down (or lie together) and communicate about their sex lives. Curiosity and frustrations about sex often do not get aired at home, where they should be aired. "If the communication about sex at home is good, overall communication usually takes care of itself," said Rona Lee Cohen, of the Seminars on Sexuality. "Yet what we see is little communication among partners, especially in the area of sexuality." If sex is basically comfortable and successful, people tend to keep their fingers crossed in hope that it will continue that way. If the relationship does not meet the mutual needs of the partners, an ostrich-like approach often develops. This results in the gradual erosion of sexual satisfaction so common to couples in their thirties and forties.

Keep the sexual lines of communication open, and the short circuits in the marriage will be fewer and farther apart. Close the channels and the chances increase dramatically that another line will be opened shortly—outside the marriage. Just be selective about when you talk about sex with your spouse. Set ground rules for that, because a lot of people share the attitude of one woman who told me, "My midwestern upbringing taught me not to talk about sex; therefore it is

hard even with my husband, especially the morning after."
If the lines of communication have been clogged for years,
open them slowly, but try to open them.

Sex Is Forever

Early in my ministry I had a long, frank discussion about
marriage with a colleague in his sixties who had been married
longer than I had been alive. He was so honest and direct
when we talked about sexual matters that I felt comfortable
asking him what it was like having sex with his wife after
thirty-two years of marriage. He smiled and answered, "Well,
it may be hard for you to understand at your age [I was
twenty-eight], but sex with my wife is still great. As a matter
of fact, it is better, a heck of a lot better—not as frequent, but
better." I'll never forget his sage and personal testimony. In
my naiveté, I had accepted the myth that sex for a man was all
downhill after his early twenties and that sex in the middle
sixties occurred only in the realm of fantasy or at least hardly
ever took place. As a young person it was hard to imagine
"old people" having sex, let alone being adventuresome and
enjoying it.

If I needed any more convincing, it came a couple of years
later when I called on a ninety-three-year-old gentleman at a
hospital in Los Angeles. I walked into his room expecting to
see a man in bed, waiting for the last rites, only to find him
doing touching-the-toe exercises. We discussed his health, and
I asked what kept him so vital and fit. His answer was a
surprising delight: "My wife is ninety-one, we are both in
good health, and it is due to daily exercise, fresh water, and
sex once a week."

I believe that sex with one partner over many years can
be rewarding, that sex when you're young isn't necessarily
better, and that having sexual relations into old age is a real
possibility for many married couples. Both my friend and his
wife in Kansas City and the ninety-year-olds from Los Angeles

had grown old gracefully, in part because they valued their sexual relationship and they were "man and woman before each other, naked and beautiful. They had no shame—their bodies were perfect. No bad parts, they were all good. They fit together perfectly."

CHAPTER 13

Creating the Climate for an Affair-Proof Marriage

"He tried to buy me happiness," said Julie, the estranged wife of an insurance company executive, "but he never woke up to what I needed. The Mercedes, the tennis club membership, the charge cards on Rodeo Drive, and the winter and summer vacations were nice to have, but he honestly thought that was enough to keep me happy as his wife. I tried telling him that what I needed—closeness, warmth, appreciation—didn't cost anything, but he wasn't willing to give that of himself."

In an era of marital emptiness amidst material plenty, Julie's frustration typifies the feeling of countless married people today. Tangible expressions of love are usually appreciated because they symbolize thoughtfulness and provide instant gratification, but such material offerings do not satisfy for very long or in any deep sense in most marriages. A successful relationship demands something much more basic—what I've termed emotional nutrients—and that will be the focus of this chapter.

The goal I pursue with couples is for each spouse to take responsibility for nurturing an atmosphere in which emotional needs are met and personal self-esteem is central to the relationship. *Therein lies the bedrock of affair prevention, for when both partners like themselves—and each other—the emotional climate is warm, loving, giving, and mutually enriching.* This perspective is nicely articulated by Father John Powell, who writes in his book *Unconditional Love*: "There is one need so fundamental, so essential that if it is met, everything else will almost certainly harmonize in a general sense of well being. When this need is properly nourished, the whole human organism will be healthy and the person will be happy. This need is a true and deep appreciation of oneself, a genuine and joyful self-acceptance, an authentic self-esteem, which results in an interior sense of celebration: It is good to be me. . . . I am very happy to be me."

Feeling good about oneself does not eliminate the need for other prevention ideas I've discussed in this book, but since most of us define who we are by how others see us, it is obvious that when we receive emotional nutrients from our spouse, this encourages us to work harder at our marriage and makes us far less inclined to seek someone else who will meet unfulfilled needs. When these nutrients are missing in a marriage, I often hear the following lament, as voiced by the mother of two young boys: "My husband is so damn wrapped up in his work that all he can think of is his money, his big-deal car, his new running shoes, and money-market certificates. He doesn't pay attention to the meal I cook, my yardwork, or the work I do around the house; I can't even get him to notice me when I walk around naked in front of him. The little trinkets he gives me as peace offerings aren't very effective anymore."

This comment is typical of many people who have let their marriage deteriorate to the point where an emotional chill permeates the household. Greetings become perfunctory, kisses of hello and goodbye meaningless rituals, conversations abrupt and stilted, and sexual relations irregular and unpleasing. Compared with this is the presumed perfection of an affair—the warmth in a lover's apartment or mountain cabin and the appreciation that is an elemental part of the atmosphere.

If there's an emotional chill in your marriage, perhaps the following suggestions—which I will expand on in this chapter—might begin the thawing process and diminish the appeal of an affair:

- Affirm rather than disaffirm your spouse.
- Guarantee mutual respect by offering respect and dignity to your partner.
- Remember the "ness" needs: kindness, goodness, closeness, and togetherness.
- Appreciate the ordinariness of your spouse.
- Value all aspects of love: lust, Eros, philia, and agape.

A.A.A. (Affirmation, Appreciation, Acclamation)

"There has never been a guy more ripe for an affair than Dennis," said a good friend of mine as we discussed our concern about a mutual acquaintance. "Sally [his wife] constantly tears him down and the poor guy can't win. She is never positive about anything. She's on him about his 'boring and unfulfilling' job, his lack of motivation around home, even his golf game. Everything he does or tries to do gets squelched, and he's so upset he wonders 'Why the hell should I keep coming home?' "

Sally and Dennis had been married for thirteen years. He worked in the family business and was proud of the job he had done to help the company grow while keeping his family his top priority. When I had a chance to talk to him privately, he told me he had no intention of destroying his marriage, but that his wife's constant negativism had weakened his commitment to fidelity—and if the right woman came along he might be tempted. Dennis, who was forty-four and not very appealing to younger women, admitted that it would be tough for him to find the special person who would reinforce his personal worth. Yet he was intent on finding that woman, unless Sally began to show her appreciation for his role as the breadwinner and to affirm him rather than destroy his self-esteem with her incessant critical remarks.

The three A's—affirmation, appreciation, and acclamation—are so critical to the well-being of any marriage that constant repetition of the theme "You are okay" is often needed. The father of a good friend from Massachusetts, a well-respected physician who fell in love with another woman after a long marriage, told me that he firmly believes it is no longer enough just to simply avoid being negative in the home; people must over-correct and constantly be in tune with positive things they can say and do. "I know many men at the top who are lonely in the sense they do not have anyone to talk to about their feelings or who will talk to them about personal matters. They are discouraged from opening up at home by wives who would rather bitch than understand, and they can't go to male subordinates at work, so many of them turn to younger women who listen carefully and who tell them 'You are wonderful, you are grey at the temples, you are terrific.' These guys succumb easily to this flattery because they are hearing things they have not heard from a woman in a long time."

Married partners can affirm each other in many ways, verbally and nonverbally. I have found that just the simple phrase "I love you" still remains the most effective way of telling a spouse how special he or she is, and yet this is often hard for people to say after years of marriage. A man I know who had been tempted to stray on several out-of-town business trips said he had rarely heard those words expressed by his wife in fourteen years of marriage. "When I ask her if she loves me, she usually says yes, but she never says it on her own initiative."

The importance of love language must not be overlooked. Those who've had affairs continually remind me that a verbalization of positive feelings is constant in their relationship and that the continual massaging of their egos with well-chosen words contributes to a special feeling. Must a marriage be any different? Words can hurt, but they can also heal, and *words of positive reinforcement can redirect a marriage that is on a collision course with an affair.*

Affirmation can also come through body language and nonverbal communication, especially "touch magic." The words may be saying "I love you," but if the face communicates anger, boredom, or disapproval, the words may be nullified. If you have difficulty expressing your love for your spouse verbally, learn to use your hands to transmit the feeling that he or she is important to you and that you desire closeness. *Touching time is prime time in any relationship,* for it brings a reassurance that "I am worthy enough to be touched"—a feeling all men and women enjoy and need. I'm not necessarily talking about the touching that leads to sex, but the little hugs and squeezes, the arm around the shoulder, the hand that is extended to give support and transmit warmth. When couples are angry at each other, a commonly heard line is "Don't come near me—don't touch me." These words hurt deeply because the power of touch is so great. So to continually deny your spouse this touch approval or to wear an invisible sign that says "Hands off" or "Don't touch" is to openly invite an affair, because people need and love to touch.

The importance of touch in a marriage has been brought home to me many times, in particular by a couple who were close to ending their eleven-year marriage. With counseling and time they were able to reconcile their difficulties, and one night they decided to go out to dinner. "There we were, just the two of us," the wife told me. "John and I were alone for the first time in months. The kids were home with a sitter we trusted, and we really felt free. He looked at me across the table, reached out, touched my hand, and played with the wedding ring he had given me. His touch was wonderful, and it made me feel good all over—about myself and about our marriage. Just to have him touch me like that meant so much."

Mutual Respect

When a marriage works well, it is usually because each spouse constantly offers the other respect and dignity. All of us have the need to be respected, and Connie was no different. Divorced from a husband who, she said, "wanted to own me like a piece of property," she recalled how she never received any respect for the decisions she made in the home, for her ideas and style, or for her work as a volunteer in her church and community. As a result of her husband's indifference, she sought to affirm her worth by having a series of romantic relationships, two of which included sex. "I finally went to bed with these other men when I felt they respected me for who I was; they made me feel that what I had to say mattered. That was all I had to hear." *We all love to hear that someone respects us because of what we do, but even more encouraging is the affirmation that someone respects us for who we are.*

One afternoon I had a delightful talk with three members of my congregation whose combined marital longevity was ninety-six years. Marion Baker, Dick Montgomery, and Roger Jayne are all in their early sixties, and when I asked them about the qualities that made their marriages strong, Marion answered for her friend Dick, whom she had known well for several years. "Dick," she said, "I admire you for several reasons, but one in particular: you have given Mary her complete dignity." All three friends agreed that they did not always like their spouse's behavior, nor did they always sympathize with particular ideas, but they always respected that partner's right to have his or her own opinion. "To put your spouse down," said Marion, "is to deny his dignity."

When these key ingredients—respect and dignity—serve as ballast for the marriage, they ensure that the relationship can tolerate differences in interests, sexual and emotional needs, and a variety of individual pursuits. In fact, many affairs could be prevented if men and women felt secure in who they are, and if they communicated that feeling of self-worth to their partners. There's nothing wrong with saying, "I think you'd be foolish to risk losing me for someone else. What we have together is too good." Some people cannot make such statements because they do not have enough self-esteem to believe it themselves. Yet most of us want to live with a partner who is emotionally secure and who projects that confidence.

The "Ness" Needs

In this sophisticated era, when specialists are able to analyze and dissect marriages through comprehensive analytical systems, and the jargon of interpersonal relationships includes phrases such as "getting it all together," "I'm okay," "do your own thing," and "being in tune," it is easy for plain, simple words we associate with Grandma's era to lose their impact. Nevertheless, I offer kindness, goodness, closeness, and togetherness as four significant allies in our defense against affairs.

Kindness and goodness are not glamorous qualities, but they endure because they work. Counselor Bob Iles told me that he feels "marital partners want loving relations with someone who makes them feel good." We feel best when someone we care about is simply kind or good to us. Long remembered is that gesture of remembrance on the birthday or anniversary, that special cup of soup when a cold has you down, that favorite meal prepared the night before a business trip, that offering to feed the kids and put them to bed when your spouse has been stuck at home all day. Do an act of kindness once a day, and you will never be without family and friends who love you.

Closeness and togetherness are ordinary qualities that most people grow to expect but rarely work to make happen once a marriage settles into its year-to-year routine. As a result, the statement "I just don't feel close to my spouse anymore" often signals a receptiveness to somebody outside the marriage. Many couples readily admit that, by design or habit, they simply do not spend time being close in quiet, simple ways. We live in an action-oriented culture of "movers and shakers," and spending time with one's spouse just sitting, reading, touching, looking at the sunset—without any other goal in mind—is often perceived as wasted time. Usually, we are consumed by activities: cleaning the house, working in the yard, getting our exercise, car pooling the kids, talking on the telephone, going out to parties or dinners, and "doing something constructive." And what suffers is that special time of being close together as husband and wife—and the reassuring feeling that can bring. Once again we can learn by looking in on lovers, who cherish just being close. (I believe that sex is often sought as a means of simply being close to another human being, regardless of the sexual satisfaction gained. As Dr. Shirley Zussman, a New York psychotherapist, points out: "We find that it isn't the sex act a woman is missing at all, but the cuddling, the closeness, and warmth that go with it.")

Often we make a common error in life—and especially in marriage—by overlooking the obvious. We know in our hearts that we are attracted to people who have the qualities that make us feel good, yet how often do we reciprocate by offering kindness, goodness, and closeness to our spouse as a regular part of our daily life?

Appreciate the Ordinary

As you try to develop and maintain an emotional climate at home so inviting that you or your spouse is not tempted to leave it for another person, do not neglect yet another old-fashioned characteristic of a sensitive married person: *the ability to love your spouse for his or her ordinary qualities.* Very few of us marry superstars, and few of us are super parents or super spouses all the time, even though we may wear tee shirts or drink from coffee cups that tell us we are. When we understand this about our marriage and we learn to appreciate the ordinary qualities we all have, we gain a valuable perspective on the unrealistic appeal of an affair. The unknown person outside our marriage—judged from a distance—can easily have a greater appeal than a well-known partner, but every single human being has his or her ordinariness.

Knowing this, happily married couples build their relationship not around the glamorous, the unusual, or the expensive, but the common characteristics we are taught as children, only to somehow cast aside as adults. These couples often speak of two ordinary words that are habitually used in their household—"please" and "thank you"—in relation to the hum-drum daily routine of making beds, fixing meals, mowing the grass, raking the leaves, watering the plants, taking out the garbage, doing laundry, folding socks, fixing a broken lamp, washing the dishes, and so on. They show each other their appreciation for bringing home paychecks, maintaining the household, and sharing the child-raising duties.

I've put together a brief list of ordinary qualities that can be made a part of any marriage with ease and success. Just doing some of the things on this list on a daily basis may take the chill out of your marriage permanently.

Lovers will:

always anticipate . . . needs and desires
regularly create . . . interesting settings and situations
rarely regulate . . . behavior of the other
never negate . . . the person they love
hardly hesitate . . . to offer thanks
sensitively communicate . . . feelings
daily originate . . . time for the "ness" needs

Authentic Love

At the heart of an affair-proof climate in any marriage is Victor Hugo's provocative statement "Supreme happiness of life is the conviction that we are loved." When we believe that our spouse really loves us, we find it much easier—and more rewarding—to tackle the difficulties that can arise in marriage and we are less inclined to ever seek another person for an intimate, sexual relationship. Rollo May used the term authentic love to describe the kind of love that sustains marriages over time. I also like to define it as the product of two people who speak the words of love but, more importantly, demonstrate their love by working at making their relationship successful. Rather than simply relying on those special feelings of being in love, *they combine feelings with action.* Said Dean Pittman McGehee of Houston: "Falling in love is no great feat at all; it is much like being born or breathing, and anyone can do that. However, growing in love is an art." So if affair prevention is to ultimately succeed in your marriage, pay heed to the four key components of authentic love: Eros, lust, philia, and agape. These elements interact to keep a relationship alive and well, and sacrificing one diminishes the strength of the marriage.

EROS

Eros, the Greek god of love, has been worshipped and sought after by men and women for centuries. This is often the most highly valued part of authentic love—the falling-in-love feeling that causes a tingling sensation when that special person is near. This feeling of being in love usually does not continue full force; it ebbs and flows like the tide. Yet it can be reawakened in marriages in which it has been dormant for years. Judith Viorst provided the right perspective when she wrote: "One advantage of marriage, it seems to me, is that when you fall out of love with him, or he falls out of love with you, it keeps you together until you maybe fall in love again."

The mistake so many couples make is placing too much emphasis on the magic of Eros and thinking that their relationship is over when they "fall out of love." Although Eros is important, we must remember that it is only one-fourth of authentic love and it alone cannot usually sustain a marriage. All too often, unfortunately, married partners trust only their feeling of "in-loveness" to describe their happiness—and to justify having an affair. People who judge their marital union exclusively on feelings like this—"When in love all is well, when not in love all is lost"—immediately set themselves up to be disappointed and also short-circuit their marriage. A more realistic approach is to pursue Eros in your marriage but be aware of its elusive nature and please do not view its absence as a signal to seek an affair.

LUST

The concept of lust has fallen on hard times. One is said to have bad taste for admitting to excessive, unrestrained sexual craving for another person, especially if that person is not one's spouse. Even lusting in one's heart has been perceived as evil by many since the time of Jesus. However, I firmly believe that feelings are neither right nor wrong, so *the feeling of lust can have an important place in your marriage.* Having a strong feeling of passion for your spouse will bring a kind of boldness to your relationship that is often only present in "first love" romances and extramarital affairs.

"I just wish my husband would occasionally throw his arms around me, sweep me off my feet, and make wild, passionate love," remarked a forty-five-year-old woman. "He used to get so excited to see me that he would rush in the door and act like a fool, but I loved it." This woman thought she wanted the passion of a young lover, but what she really yearned for more than anything was the same response from her husband.

Lusting after an "ordinary" spouse with whom you share toothpaste, dental floss, and a bathroom glass may not be as appealing as lusting after a young and uninhibited new body. But unexpected dividends often occur when a couple that have a history together reintroduce lust into their marriage. Unbridled passion for life and for your spouse is a marvelous attitude. Exuberance and enthusiasm are the hallmarks of lust and, when regularly shared with your spouse, will greatly diminish the appeal of having this component of love met elsewhere.

PHILIA

A commonly devalued part of authentic love, but the core of many successful marriages, is brotherly love (philia), or "buddy love," as I like to describe it. The love shared between brothers and sisters or between close friends has an enduring quality that belongs in every marriage. As my ninety-year-old grandmother said about her fifty-six-year marriage: "Poppy and I were always best of friends. I loved him like a brother."

Love, as I said earlier, is something that happens between two people, and it is expressed by friendship. Friendship includes sacrifice—and the ultimate expression of authentic love must involve sacrifice. How much you are willing to sacrifice for your spouse is a good indicator of your level of authentic love; what you are willing to sacrifice shows how loyal you are. Most often we see this love expressed between buddies. Erich Fromm, in *The Art of Loving,* states that "love is the active concern for the life and growth of that which we love." Living this out in your marriage and placing a premium on philia will surely strengthen the emotional climate in your marriage.

AGAPE

An enduring marriage is bound by a fervent belief in agape—an unconditional, "in sickness and in health" kind of love. Granted, we may often have to struggle to gracefully accept the displeasing, unlovable characteristics of our spouse. Sometimes we fail, as typified by the woman who was in the process of divorcing her husband and who told me, "I have to love my husband, but I just can't; there are too many things about him that I no longer like." Loving unconditionally is, in fact, the mark of saints, but if we can aspire to this level of selfless love, we will be aspiring to the most valuable element of authentic love.

Agape is love with no strings attached and without concern for a payoff or a reward. As such, it goes against human nature, for when we do something nice and loving for someone we expect to be loved in return. But agape is the kind of love that will carry you and your spouse through the crossroads of your marriage. Just at the point when your displeasure is the greatest, you will need to love most fully, and selfless agape may pull you through. Without that kind of dedication in those times of greatest distance, anger, or annoyance, you will possibly leave your marriage open to a third person who may be able to alleviate personal anguish and become the object of all your loving capabilities.

When your partner knows that he or she is loved during the hard times of the marriage—when you extend that extra care, attention, and understanding even though it cannot be returned at that moment—the pleasure for both of you is magnified many times. *Happiness is indeed the conviction that we are loved by a spouse—unconditionally.*

Dr. Will Menninger gave the world Menninger Time, and he also said repeatedly, "Love cures. It cures those who give it, and it cures those who receive it." The kind of love he speaks of is within the grasp of all couples, although it can easily slip away if it is not nourished and cherished. Loving is an art, requiring blood, sweat, and tears; it does not just happen, and we must give it our constant attention if we want it to work its power in our marriage.

Growing in love in a marriage marks the maturity of the relationship. Love is a process that never really ends. And when you work to balance lust, Eros, philia, and agape, you will provide your marriage with an emotional warmth and strength that can last a lifetime.

CHAPTER 14

The Role of Religion in Preventing Affairs

To help broaden my understanding of affairs, I wrote to more than fifty people in the helping professions across the United States. Among the letters I received back, I enjoyed the insights of Diane Cooley, a member of The Commission on Human Sexuality for the Episcopal Diocese of Los Angeles. She wrote, "Continuing assistance and support by the church after the marriage ceremony might be an extra service to husbands and wives. Such constancy of concern and encouragement by the church might assist couples to explore, expand, and emphasize the values and benefits of marriage—as well as attempt to help them resolve any problems accompanying their infidelity, if it occurs."

Is it realistic to assume that the church can play a positive role in affair prevention? My answer is a definite yes. I believe rabbis, priests, and ministers can help married couples elevate fidelity to a major goal and that the clergy can indeed learn to discuss affairs from an informed point of view. The churches and synagogues of our nation are uniquely suited for dealing with tough issues of life such as divorce and affairs; these issues require people to affirm acceptance, forgiveness, love, and understanding as cornerstones of reconciliation—and the church is committed to that as a prime goal. The leaders of our religious institutions are certainly capable of providing a firm foundation of accurate, well-presented information about human sexuality in general, and marriage specifically.

Having said this, I want to emphasize that I am not naively assuming that the church is always up to date. I have a letter from a clergyman in Chicago who wrote, "The longer I live, the more I distrust institutions. I feel the church has too narrow a view on extramarital involvement and it all too often creates hypocrisy and unnecessary pain." Right or wrong, this attitude reflects the sentiments of many people who feel the church has not presented an enlightened, well-informed story to its members when it comes to human sexuality. I know that many people in fact regard the church as the last place to turn for help in a marital crisis, especially if there is a sexual problem.

Still, the church has the basic material, structure, and people to be of great help to married couples. What it must work on, however, is its presentation. Waving the finger of righteous indignation at the lack of morals in society or raising the stern hand of repressive parent helps very few people and alienates nearly everyone. I sense that the vast majority of my parishioners believe that adultery is wrong, even when they are among the guilty. Therefore, any efforts to mold their behavior from the pulpit by invoking fear or punishment will probably fall on deaf ears.

Another important step is for us church leaders to "get our sexuality act together." We must be sensitive to our own sexuality and aware of the unrefuted fact that, like everyone else, we are faced with and may succumb to the temptations of an affair. By coming out of our religious ivory towers and casting off our holier-than-thou attitude, we can offer greater respectability and gain greater trust among the laity. The hypocrisy of "don't do as I do, but do as I say" has no place in our religious institutions. Clergy of all faiths are not expected to be experts on sex—or perfect in their behavior—but are expected to honestly and openly approach the subject that is so central to the well-being of any society.

A good place for a clergyperson to begin is with the Bible. We open the Bible and turn to the Ten Commandments found in the Book of Exodus. Number seven is "Thou shalt not commit adultery." Turning to the Book of Deuteronomy, we find "Do not commit adultery" (5:18), "Do not desire another man's wife . . . or anything else he owns" (5:20), and "If a man is caught having intercourse with another man's wife both of them are to be put to death. In this way you will get rid of this evil" (22:22). These are strong words with a clear message, and such biblical admonitions have been allies to many people who have sought to remain faithful during marriage. These laws of the Torah, the first five books of the Bible, have in fact been sufficient in and of themselves to deter many would-be adulterers or adulteresses.

"Having an affair is an act totally against God's will and our beliefs," said a young married woman in my church. "If you truly love one another, the temptations of others shall not overtake you." We may applaud Marcie's statement, we may laugh in disbelief, we may say "right on, lady," or we may snicker at her apparent naiveté. However, we should recognize that the biblical prescriptions for living are a guiding influence in many marriages in our country. The Reverend Joe Rhodes, a Christian counselor and minister, speaks for many when he says, "Adultery is not just a sin against another person, or a group of people, which it is. Adultery is also a sin against God." Strong religious commitment, faith, and practice have been and will continue to be an effective deterrent to affairs—especially when combined with some of the practical suggestions offered in this book.

As we explore the scriptures further, we see that neither biblical nor talmudic (commentaries on the Torah) literature contains a specific term for sex. Yet Judaism believes that moderation and self-control in sex is the essence of holiness. Recognition that man has a sex drive and that this drive is not sinful or shameful is an important teaching. There is also a strong emphasis on family in the Scriptures, and sex that is perceived as destroying family is condemned. Rape, incest, premarital promiscuity, and extramarital sex all fall under the heading of "capable of destroying families." This is an important point to remember, for it means that a discussion of adultery fits into any discussion of the human family— and the roots of this concept trace back to the beginnings of recorded history. *Adultery has never been condoned by the religious community and probably never will be, partly because it has the potential of breaking down families.*

In biblical law, extramarital intercourse by a married man is not per se a crime. This arises from the Old Testament concept of marriage in which the woman was viewed as a man's possession. Adultery by a woman was disapproved of because it was violation of the husband's right to have sole sexual possession of his wife and to be assured that his children were his. An adulteress is described in Proverbs as one who seeks the protection of night and possesses a "smooth tongue to lure the foolish like oxen to the slaughter." We are also warned that "traffic with adulterous woman leads inevitably to the loss of wealth; the adulterer is more foolish than a thief, who will at least escape with his life." We know that David committed adultery with Bathsheba, the wife of Uriah the Hittite, and he was condemned. However, a woman who committed adultery was dealt a much harsher fate. If caught, the woman was sometimes forced to drink a special liquid which would somehow conclusively prove her unfaithfulness. Often she was stoned to death (sometimes with her lover) because this was the punishment prescribed for crimes that threatened the stability of the family. The prophet Ezekiel warns, "They will stir up a crowd to stone you and they will cut you to pieces with their swords."

Over the centuries, of course, the church has invoked the Bible to frighten people out of affairs with its "thou shalt nots," its method of dealing with transgressors, the fear of damnation, and the fear of a judgmental God who will separate the black sheep from the white sheep come Judgment

Day. Your own behavior may not be affected by these religious admonitions, but many people feel that such fear is the only method of affair prevention that has worked for them.

I feel, however, that in this day and age perhaps the most effective prevention aid the church or synagogue can offer its constituents is an honest appraisal of human sexuality.

First, when the church can offer positive reinforcement to that which is good about sex, people will have a much greater willingness to listen to what the church has to say about the potential negative and disruptive elements of irresponsible sex (e.g., extramarital affairs). Human sexuality is central to the lives of most men and women, and enlightened presentations by the church can help adults make informed decisions. Also, helping people discover how responsible sex can, and should, be a meaningful part of their marriage may in turn decrease the need to seek extramarital sexual partners. Attempts by the church to control sexual behavior through fear may eventually prove self-defeating by driving off those who could benefit from an honest, open dialogue about marriage and sex.

Second, the church must broadly proclaim the value of emotional and sexual fidelity in marriage. Attention should be given to those people who have had strong, healthy, life-affirming marriages so that there are positive models for other couples. In recent years, a prime example of this reinforcement for marraige and family stability has been the highly successful Marriage Encounter programs offered through Protestant, Jewish, and Catholic faiths.

Third, the church should aid in affair prevention by refusing to cast the first stone. The church has the option to condemn and ostracize those who commit adultery, and I know men and women who have been evicted from their church or church positions because of such behavior. But such action by the church merely reinforces its public image as an unrelenting moralist. Who are we to judge behavior and act as jury? Let us look at a well-known biblical story that supports my point here.

> They went each to his own house, but Jesus went to the Mount of Olives. Early in the morning he came again to the temple; all the people came to him, and he sat down and taught them. The scribes and the Pharisees brought a woman who had been caught in adultery, and placing her in the midst they said to him, "Teacher, this woman has been caught in the act of adultery. Now in the law Moses commanded us to stone such. What do you say about her?" This they said to test him, that they might have some charge to bring against him. Jesus bent down and wrote with his finger on the ground. And as they continued to ask him, he stood up and said to them, "Let him who is without sin among you be the first to throw a stone at her." And once more he bent down and wrote with his finger on the ground. But when they heard it, they went away, one by one, beginning with the eldest, and Jesus was left alone with the woman standing before him. Jesus looked up and said to her, "Woman, where are they? Has no one condemned you?" She said, "No one, Lord." And Jesus said, "Neither do I condemn you; go, and do not sin again."

Casting rocks at people who have had troubles in their marriage or who have flirted with the idea of adultery by lusting in their hearts will only enhance the likelihood that they will turn away from the church. *The door must always remain open someplace in society for those people who feel cut off and alone and sinful.* The church's doors are hinges that open in and open out simultaneously; acceptance rather than condemnation will keep people coming in those doors. As Reverend Mid Wooten, from Windsor, N.C., stated, "God intends people to grow close through community. The synagogue or church can provide genuine and deep relationships, a sense of caring, and a love which every person needs."

Fourth, in a world hungry for stability and guidance, the church can provide a wonderful life-support system for many people. Our Judeo-Christian heritage offers all of us something positive to live for: the worth of each individual, marriage, the family unit, fidelity, relationships based on promise and covenant, and forgiveness and acceptance when people fall short of the ideals they have set for themselves. By affirming that which is good and that which brings a sense of well-being, the church can offer an environment that is safe and accepting, and which then encourages personal growth. However, at no other time in history has it been as important as now for the church to stand up and be counted as a powerful ally to those who are striving to make their familial relations work better. The church—through its clergy and laity—should be at the forefront of the belief so eloquently stated by James Michener in his novel *Chesapeake*: "It is testimony that is needed: A human being, to live a meaningful life . . . must at critical moments testify publicly as to fundamental beliefs."

Men and women everywhere should publicly proclaim their commitment to essential marital values without reservation, with boldness, and with confidence. If you stand with others who are honestly committed to the principles of affair prevention, you stand in good company.

CHAPTER 15

Coping with Affairs After the Fact

No system devised for affair prevention is foolproof, and no marriage is totally immune. We know that even well-intentioned, deeply religious, happily married people have affairs.

Affair prevention may come too late to some of you reading this book. Perhaps you are in the middle of an affair that is still unknown to your spouse and you are wondering "How do I get out of this mess?" Or perhaps your affair has already come to light—or you have discovered your spouse is involved in one. Whatever the case, you are looking for after-the-fact guidelines to help you deal maturely with this crisis in your marriage.

This chapter will deal with many of the issues involved, but my first assumption is that no advice will help you if you do not really want help or you do not want to save your marriage. My second assumption is that if you are receptive to counsel, I think this advice can help ease you through the long hours of soul-searching that accompany the discovery of an affair.

When Your Affair Is Undisclosed or Undiscovered

If you are involved in an affair, *search your soul to determine what value the relationship has to you.* An honest look should dictate your next step. If you realize the affair is temporary and not particularly rewarding and your marriage still has top priority, you may choose not to tell your spouse. As psychiatrist Dr. Anthony Rosenthal states, "It seems beneficial for the wife or husband not to know in many situations; so ask yourself, are you sure you want to drag your spouse into this?" I never advise a person that he or she necessarily tell, but I've found that it is often easier to work with a couple toward marital reconciliation when the affair has been revealed with no intention to hurt.

If you are in the midst of an unidentified and undisclosed affair, *seek the counsel of a person you trust*—and try to listen objectively to his or her advice. The problem here, as I mentioned earlier in the book, is that people enjoying an affair rarely choose to listen to an outsider's counsel. But you may have reached the point where you are totally confused and going crazy from the whole process of trying to hide your activities from your spouse and you may greatly benefit by unburdening yourself with another person.

Here are some other questions to ask yourself as you try to come to grips with your affair:

- How is this extramarital relationship affecting your personal well-being? Is it making you a more loving person—or one more hateful and spiteful?
- How do you feel about violating your marriage vows or giving in to the collective pressure to "live life fully" by having an affair?
- What do your actions tell you about your ability to maintain a committed relationship to one person?
- Do you view your affair as a violation, or as recreation?
- Is this a two-way street? How would you react if your spouse were having a similar affair?
- What effect would public disclosure of your affair have on the significant others in your life (e.g., friends, relatives, business associates, church members)?

How honest have you been with your lover? Are you offering the prospect of an ongoing relationship and promising to do things that you cannot deliver (i.e., that you will marry some day, when in truth you have no intention of divorcing your spouse)?

Hearing the answers to these and other questions you might pose may not be rewarding to you because they could hurt. However, when you can step back like this and confront your actions, you lessen the chances of developing a pattern of extramarital involvement. People have admitted to me that once they had an affair and got away with it unscathed, without any real soul-searching or discovery, the next one seemed easier to handle. Bishop William Temple called this process "the narcotic effect of sin." He said, "As soon as we have done something that is nasty, we have blunted our own capacity to be disgusted. We have tarnished the mirror in which we are to look at our own reflection."

When Your Spouse's Affair Comes to Light

No magical ointment can ease the pain and trauma that result when a spouse discovers that his or her partner has been cheating. An affair affects the emotions differently from any other event in a marriage, and it is almost impossible for the uninvolved spouse to remain objective in the face of what has been revealed. If you are in this situation, nobody is expecting you to remain detached as you try to work through the crisis. And closing your eyes or running away will not make the affair vanish into thin air. So what to do? Here are some steps to consider.

1. *Discover, if possible, the degree of involvement and the level of commitment your spouse has to his or her lover.*

Is the affair an immediate threat to the marriage? Are the bags packed, the bank accounts juggled, your pictures returned? Is the apartment rented? Is all talk centering on how fast your spouse can get out of your sight?

Or is the end of the marriage not immediate, but the affair was of such intensity that you see the repercussions as a continuing problem? Does your spouse normally avoid acting on impulse and does the pattern established in the affair indicate that it will probably take a long time to resolve?

What is the pattern of your spouse's extramarital behavior? Have you discovered a blossoming affair, or a relationship that is already dying? Did you just happen to stumble across a one-night stand or a series of transient sexual encounters? Perhaps once was enough to get the mystery or fantasy out of your spouse's system.

Answers to questions like these may not be easily forthcoming, but as you try to reach a level of reconciliation, it is vital that you ascertain as best you can the degree of your spouse's involvement and where the third person stands in relation to your marriage.

2. *If you still love your spouse—but disapprove of his or her behavior—do not abandon ship prematurely.* Even if you come home to discover a note on top of the diapers that says "I have gone to Tahiti with your best friend, Suzy," do not give up if you still think the marriage is viable. Suzy may sunburn easily or she may not like your husband's snoring, and he may soon be back asking for a new start. Of course, if his absence persists you may be kidding yourself by holding out hope. You may also truly feel that your spouse is a jerk and you're not about to expend any energy to save the marriage. It is your choice.

3. *Do not ever introduce violence into an already volatile situation.* Your frustration may make you want to throw something or hit your spouse over the head with a bat, but violence will only serve as a catalyst for ending the marriage and reaffirming your spouse's reasons for wanting to get away from you. In a similar sense, be careful how you handle your feelings of betrayal, anger, resentment, and bitterness. They demand release, but do not inflict pain on your children or friends for the anger felt toward your spouse. Pay a pro-

fessional for that kind of unloading. It's unhealthy to hold
your feelings in completely, and when you express them with
a responsible listener, long-term benefits will be maximized.

4. *If you desire to save your marriage, avoid issuing
ultimatums and threats, such as "I'll get you for this."* Vindictive comments roll off the tongue so easily when one's ego has
been bruised or shattered. You may see your spouse as a hor-
ribly rotten person for having done this to you, but threats
and warnings will simply push him or her away from you. Remember, too, that in many situations a marriage is already
on shaky ground prior to the affair and certainly on crumbling
ground after the affair has been discovered. So it is wise not
to push your spouse out too abruptly by ill-chosen diatribes
that are not easily forgotten.

5. *Trying to answer the question "Who is to blame?"
will only block the process of reconciliation.* Even if blame
can be proved, the real reasons lie with both partners, so to
get bogged down arguing this issue delays progress toward
reconstructing a mutually satisfying marriage. Of course, my
advice goes against human nature. Both spouses are always
quick to place blame for an affair squarely on the other's
shoulder. The uninvolved mate naturally blames the one who
committed adultery, while the one who had the affair accuses
the other of creating an untenable marriage environment.
In either case, you will only widen the already expanding gulf
between you and your partner by pointing a finger and
declaring "You are the cause of all this misery."

6. *There's nothing to be gained by telling every person
you know that your spouse has had an affair and that he or she
is a bad person.* Once again, the temptation may be to let
all your friends know about your spouse's behavior as a way of
compensating for your hurt, but seeking revenge in this manner will come back to haunt your marriage—and will often
produce a personal guilt that is difficult to erase. The need
to talk and tell is great, and it is an important release valve,
but be selective about your confidants. You are dealing with

a private matter that should basically remain private, so choose a person you can trust, who cares, and who will keep his or her mouth shut.

7. *A friend may be a good listening post, but avoid asking for prescriptions, because the answers must come from you.* When your self-esteem has been badly shaken, it is common to want to turn to a friend for the a's, b's, and c's of "what do I do now?" Good friends will offer advice and their counsel may be well-intentioned and well-informed, but it may also distill down to "You poor thing—he wasn't worth much anyway" or "You've been henpecked long enough—this is your ticket out of a bad deal." In a situation like this, the hurt spouse is like a numb sponge who will soak up advice from any source. Turn to a friend who will listen, but try to rely on trained counselors for advice; or better still, with a counselor's help, discover the advice within yourself.

Where to Turn for Help

It takes a strong person to be able to ask for help, especially when you have to admit to another person that your spouse has been cheating on you. Most of us, men especially, have been raised in the "I can and I will" school of personal growth, and turning to others to help us solve our problems is often seen as a sign of weakness. In fact, making that call to a people-helper may be one of the most difficult things you have ever had to do. But *I truly believe you are a strong person when you ask for help*—and not a weak person, as we have been led to believe.

There are countless people-helpers ready and willing to offer their generally sage advice and counsel, yet how does one cut through this plethora of counselors and increase the odds of finding a person who will be helpful? (Later in the chapter I will discuss couples therapy.)

An overall guiding principle is my firm belief that if you have been stung by the discovery of your spouse's affair, you need a counselor who can be trusted and who will take a genuine interest in you. If you know a minister, priest, or rabbi, turn to him for comfort and perhaps for the name of an expert who is a good listener, a caring person, and a competent counselor. A clergyperson who is in tune with the needs of his constituency will know a number of qualified men and women who have exhibited the skills I cited above. Ask the referring person if he has received feedback from anyone he has sent to a particular counselor.

I am well aware that many people do not have an institutional religious affiliation or a friend in the clergy. If this is true for you, then be prepared to ask your prospective counselor some tough questions about his training, credentials, and experience. You are going to pay him good money to help you with a difficult problem, and you should be confident that you've picked a good person. Another crucial area to explore with this counselor is his moral outlook on life. Does he have a philosophy that is harmonious with yours? People are often dismayed by the advice they hear when they accept a counselor without doing any prior homework. In part this may be attributed to a different view of what is right and wrong or appropriate and inappropriate behavior. There are counselors who are Jewish, Buddhists, agnostics, Jesus freaks, Catholics, atheists, hedonists, Episcopalians, etc. Some will advocate a "do your own thing" style of living, others may encourage sexual exploration outside the marriage, while others will go to the opposite extreme and condone sex for procreation alone. Counselors vary greatly, so be prepared to ask for information.

After one or two visits to the counselor you have selected, take time to assess whether you feel you can trust him (or her) and benefit from his advice. If you are not really sure, do not return; you are under no obligation—except to yourself— so you may terminate at any time. However, if you do quit, make sure the reason is not because the counselor is probing areas of hurt, because that is what he should do. *Ultimately,*

*you do not go to a psychiatrist or counselor because your
spouse is having an affair. You go because something is going
on within you that you need to resolve.*

You are paying for this person's time, experience, and
care. If he does not really seem to care about you or his view
of life is way different from yours, find someone who does
care, who has similar values, and who is skillful.

Working Through the Crisis

Once the shock begins to wear off after your spouse's
affair has come to light and you have sought help, the next
step is to begin the long, hard work of resurrecting your marriage (if, of course, that is your goal). Here's where a competent counselor can help guide you in the right direction by
asking you to focus on yourself—and not on your spouse's
behavior. You may want to change your spouse's behavior, but
in the end you can change only yourself.

Bemoaning one's existence after an affair has been discovered is natural and a "woe is me" posture has been heard
countless times in counseling offices. It may feel good to un-
burden oneself in this manner, but eventually this attitude
becomes totally unproductive. A typical example was the distraught housewife—a mother of three children under the age
of six—who burst into tears the moment she was in the
privacy of my office. "How could he have done this to me?"
she cried. "How could he just pick up with this other woman
and leave us all alone?" Over the next two hours I let her
unload her frustrations, but I gradually had her focus on
how she was going to cope with the reality of the situation. I
had her zero in on the changes that were required of her as she
emerged as a "new person," without a husband but still with
her home and three children. A session that began amidst
tears of self-pity ended with her saying, "I will be able to
handle this, but it kills me to have to face my friends and
family."

I warned earlier that in the aftermath of an affair the issue will not be resolved if you take an ostrich-like approach. Confrontation and discussion with your spouse will prove much more effective than avoidance. However, as you struggle to reach the heart of the issue and as you reflect on why the affair happened, save yourself further pain by not asking to hear the minute details of your spouse's romantic involvement. Human nature being what it is, knowing about the sordid side of the story may be appealing. But questions that you may be dying to ask—Is she really good in bed? Did the two of you make love in our house? What presents did he give you?—can only produce further hurt and emotional distance. Instead of dwelling on your strong feelings of betrayal and adding new fuel, you want to do all you can to undo these feelings as best you can.

I like the example provided by a close friend whose husband had a brief sexual fling on a business trip. "I know it happened—my husband told me," she said, "but that's all I needed to know, and I asked him not to give me any more details. It would have hurt too much, even the barest outline. But believe me, we talked about everything else that had to do with *why* he did it."

Here's another important issue to consider as the hurt spouse. In many post-affair debates, the spouse who had the affair will try to tell you in no uncertain terms why the affair was solely your fault. You have already suffered enough personal pain, and I recommend that you do not accept the blame in your desire to bring about a peace treaty. You may have played a part in the affair's germination and development, but please do not allow your spouse to transfer guilt to you and deflect the focus off his or her behavior. Your spouse acted and was guilty of infidelity—not you. Also, when you refuse to accept blame and to minimize the significance of what your spouse has done, something quite mysterious may happen: *As you demand respect for your feelings, you earn respect.* When you refuse to be treated as the person who caused the affair, your partner may begin to see you in a new light. At a moment when both of you are confused and emotionally drained, your affirmative action and willingness to deal honestly with your spouse may be an unexpected source of great strength. In fact, I have known of several marriages that have survived the crisis of an affair primarily because the innocent partner confronted the situation in a strong and self-reliant but caring manner.

If you are determined to keep your marriage alive, time and patience are important allies in the aftermath of a discovered affair. Allowing time to work its magic healing process is hard if, like most of us, you are caught up in a world of instant solutions. And patience is hard to come by when your spouse's behavior poses a monumental threat to your presumed well-being. But to force the issue may not be in your best interest and to make statements such as "I know you're going to leave me for her; you wanted an excuse for years and now you have it, so go ahead and go," can act as a self-fulfilling catalyst. Your statement may reflect reality, but why reinforce what may be his feelings by putting words in his mouth? Always look for ways to buy time, for it gives both you and your spouse a chance to gain a better perspective on your marriage.

Building Trust Again

Trying to rebuild the foundation of trust that was, ideally, an essential part of your marriage is a long and demanding task for both of you. Men and women alike have great difficulty in regaining trust for a spouse who has cheated. I've often heard the statement "I really don't know if I can ever trust my partner again," and I know how real that feeling is. That fact is one of the paramount reasons I place such a strong emphasis on affair prevention. I really do not know if any counselor or friend can help a person rebuild his or her trust in a spouse. *This new sense of trust, if it develops, must come from within and must be reinforced by the subsequent actions of the guilty spouse.*

This is not to say that all hope is lost. One cannot will away an affair, but the ability to forgive and accept—a treasured part of our Judeo-Christian heritage—can begin the process of reconciliation and the reestablishment of trust. The Reverend Joe Rhodes (and many other counselors) believes that the only way a couple can begin to rebuild this trust is to clean the slate and get down to ground level. "The offending mate needs to seek forgiveness from the offended mate. But," he warns, "the unwillingness to forgive on the part of the innocent spouse may be more damaging than the act itself."

As the wounded partner, you may try to be a saintly forgiver and forgetter, but you also need the help of an understanding partner, especially in the first months or even years after the affair. Your partner will have to make extra efforts to justify your fragile trust and may have to dramatically alter old patterns, such as flirtation and nights out with the girls or boys.

Couples Counseling

After an affair has been discovered, individual counseling is the essential first step toward eventual joint counseling with your spouse. You need to ventilate your feelings through a counselor in a one-on-one situation, to work through the shock, the visceral anger, and the damage that has been done to your self-esteem. Then, after you have begun to stabilize your life and function in everyday activities, you need to step back and, with your spouse, assess whether the two of you are committed to saving the marriage.

Here is where what I call the "miracle of transformation" must occur, for it really is a miracle to me when two people can emerge from a marital crisis like this and enter counseling together with an expressed desire to make the marriage work.

Perhaps your spouse has said, "I feel terrible about what I did. I'm never going to see that person again and I now want to go into counseling with you. I'm ready to commit myself again and to really take a look at our marriage." If you can accept this peace offering and you've regained enough trust in your spouse to work hard at putting the marriage back together, then I feel the two of you will have cleared a major hurdle to reconciliation.

What so often happens, unfortunately, is that one partner wants to work on the marriage more than the other or is unwilling to face up to the sensitive issues that will be raised by a skillful therapist or counselor. And so each partner goes it alone, when the problems that brought about the affair are the responsibility of both parties—and must ultimately be tackled together, ideally with the stimulus of joint counseling.

An affair may be accurately compared to a chest cold. A chest cold may actually result in some good if it leads to a diagnosis of something unsuspected or to the prevention of something worse. So in terms of your response to a discovered affair, all the professional people with whom I have consulted warn that you should not do anything precipitous. *Wait until you really understand what is going on with your spouse before you take any drastic actions.* "The affair may be a way of acting out an internal personal problem," advises Dr. Anthony Rosenthal, "and under these circumstances it may not threaten the marriage." Often a person having an affair does not really want to leave the marriage. In some cases, a divorce—which is the gut-level solution—may not be the best solution for a particular couple. Busting up marriages has become a cultural pastime today, yet many people are finally realizing that this may not be the smartest way to handle crisis in a marriage—especially a crisis that is the direct result of an affair's coming to light.

CHAPTER 16

Your Marriage Is Worth Saving

"Monogamy is something I never really gave a great deal of thought to until recently, when rather unexpectedly but very explicitly, I got propositioned," wrote Brian Vachon, editor of *Vermont Life*, in an article for *Ms.* magazine. "It was not at all a professional offer and the woman who was making it was lovely and charming. It was not an offer I could brush off effortlessly. In fact, it was an invitation I toyed with for more than a moment. But eventually I said no; I thanked her for what I considered a very high compliment, and said—for the first time in my life—that my wife and I are into fidelity . . . we take our conventional marriage vows seriously; so thank you—really—I said, but no."

For an important moment, Brian Vachon forced himself to be still and listen to what his heart and mind were really saying; he heard a small, reasoned voice within him speaking "my marriage is worth preserving," and he gracefully withdrew from an awkward situation.

When I contemplate the future of marriage in this country, I see men and women like Brian Vachon directly challenging the tide of social pressure that propels them to extramarital involvements and often divorce. Granted, affairs will always be a viable option for some people, but I believe the great majority will find that affairs are no longer a necessary alternative to an inadequate marriage. Many men and women are already saying "Hey, my marriage may not be perfect, but divorce and the prospect of remarriage is not all that appealing either; every marriage is going to have areas of difficulty to work through. Therefore, instead of moving from one relationship to another, I'm going to develop new ways of relating to my spouse and make our marriage work."

One encouraging trend within our society today is that men and women are gaining a greater appreciation of their own worth within the marriage. This fact alone is significant in the ability of a marriage to withstand the disclosure of an affair. Realistically, affairs cause marriages to bend, and some to break. The discovery of extramarital involvement causes great pain for both partners, and the couple that tries to stick it out through the anger and distrust must undergo a traumatic experience. The overwhelming response is to want to run away and give up on the marriage, but if you find yourself in this situation, I encourage you to first take a long, hard look at your marriage. Said my friend Carole Lanning, a mother and grandmother: "Running away from a marriage really doesn't solve anything because it doesn't change any of the things you are walking away from; it just says 'I'm not going to deal with that problem.' I feel that somewhere in life, to find any kind of personal comfort, you finally have to say 'I'm not walking away anymore—I'm staying here and we're going to solve this situation.' " Without reservation, I firmly believe marriage as an institution is well worth preserving, and you may find, when you take a mature perspective, that your marriage in particular is worth preserving.

Dr. Carlfred Broderick states that infidelity can be turned into a profitable experience by a couple, but only when a combination of two things occurs: one, "despite marital hurts and resentments, there is a fundamental commitment to the marriage," and two, "through the terrific jolt which the infidelity and the discovery caused, the couple takes a new, hard look at their relationship and what they can do to revitalize it." We can safely say that most men and women value

a one-to-one living arrangement, and we must remind ourselves that the ethos of instant gratification (sexual and otherwise) which pervades our daily thought pattern should not
destroy our basic human values. Therefore, do not summarily
dismiss your spouse even if he or she has succumbed to the
lure of instant pleasure via an affair. In the same sense, be
careful not to decide on divorce simply because you have
fallen in love with somebody else. You may think you have
finally found the "right" person, but your marriage may be
able to adjust to the new demands, wants, needs, and expectations that the affair has brought to the surface.

An image that I find helpful is *the seesaw effect*, where
two married partners are on opposite ends but working toward a mutual balance in their life together. At times they are
equal and stable, while at other times one person is up and
the other down. But as long as the seesaw keeps moving, the
marriage remains relatively healthy. Keeping the marital seesaw in balance means keeping the heart (authentic love), the
spirit (emotional climate), the body (sexual relationship), and
the mind (mutually shared interests) in harmony with each
component part of one's partner. If an affair does occur in
your marriage, throwing the seesaw out of sync, remember
that it can begin to function smoothly again—over a period
of time—with work and an understanding of the reasons why
the affair took place.

In these turbulent times, when affairs are prevalent,
divorce commonplace, and the worth of human life is under
attack, one of man's enduring aspirations is still to give love
and to receive love. Many complex dynamics and dimensions
comprise a loving relationship, but I conclude this book by
offering a three-part challenge to action for your marriage:

One, you are worthy as a unique individual, capable of
finding personal meaning within the context of a loving relationship. Therefore, self-respect must be a cornerstone of that
partnership.

Two, a monogamous lifelong marital union is a worthy ideal because it offers a level of intimacy that grows over time and provides the potential for a gratifying sexual union.

Three, meaning for your life will ultimately result by sharing your life with people you value. Therefore, never discount the worth of another human being, a friend, and especially your spouse—they are the real source of personal joy and well-being.

Marriage as it exists today is not without its limitations and liabilities, and many who are married may chose to dissolve their union—to the benefit of both parties. However, for most of us, the ideal about which we dreamed the day we exchanged vows of fidelity and commitment and love "until death separates us" is still within our grasp. Through the years, practically every married couple will experience times when the towel is poised and ready to be thrown in. Resisting the tide of popular opinion and action, which says "quit and find another partner," is not easy.

The prevention, or the working through, of an affair may not be the greatest single achievement in your life, but it may go a long way toward helping you live up to the ideal you set for yourself when you were married—keeping the union alive and growing forever. When men and women are actively committed to affair prevention, they affirm how much mutual respect they have for one another and how much they value their partner. These ingredients—respect and value—can alone sustain and nourish many marriages.

Preserving your marriage may be the most personally satisfying experience of your lifetime. Good luck! May each new day bring you the peace and fulfillment that comes from being deeply committed to the sanctity of another human being—and your marriage.